Spellbound

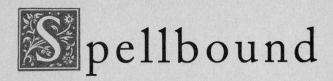

Spellbound

THE SURPRISING ORIGINS *and* ASTONISHING SECRETS *of* ENGLISH SPELLING

James Essinger

DELTA TRADE PAPERBACKS

SPELLBOUND
A Delta Book

PUBLISHING HISTORY
Robson Books hardcover edition (UK) published 2006
Delta Trade Paperback edition / May 2007

Published by
Bantam Dell
A Division of Random House, Inc.
New York, New York

Book design by Susan Hood
Photograph on p. 115 © The Ashmolean Museum

Library of Congress Cataloging-in-Publication Data
Essinger, James, 1957–
Spellbound: the surprising origins and astonishing secrets of English
spelling / James Essinger. — Delta trade pbk. ed.
p. cm.
Includes bibliographical references and index.
ISBN 978-0-385-34084-7 (trade pbk. : alk. paper)
1. English language—Orthography and spelling—History. 2. English
language—Etymology. 3. Spelling reform. I. Title.
PE1141.E86 2007
421'.52—dc22
2007001195

Printed in the United States of America
Published simultaneously in Canada

www.bantamdell.com

BVG   10 9 8 7 6 5 4 3 2 1

Dedicated to the memory of my father,

TED ESSINGER,

who loved languages

Born in Chemnitz, Germany, May 23, 1922
Died in Leicester, England, August 5, 2005

As language was at its beginning merely oral, all words of necessary or common use were spoken before they were written... The powers of the letters, when they were applied to a new language, must have been vague and unsettled, and therefore different hands would exhibit the same sound by different combinations.

—Dr. Samuel Johnson,
from the Preface to his *Dictionary of the English Language* (1755)

CONTENTS

CONTENTS

PREFACE

S*pellbound?*

Yes, because as users of the English language we're utterly bound to the most outrageous, illogical, idiosyncratic spelling system in the world.

Outrageous and illogical? Yes, absolutely. But if you look deeper at the English spelling system and how it has developed since the English language first came into being more than 1,500 years ago, *then* the way English spelling works starts to make a whole lot more sense.

But why on earth should you be interested in finding out why and how English spelling has developed?

One reason is that the story of English spelling is a terrific detective story. As well as that, understanding how English spelling has become what it is will most likely *improve your spelling*. Why? Because it will make you more sympathetic to the way English is spelled.

And there's something else. Understanding how English

spelling has evolved—and how the spelling system of English fits in with the story of writing as a whole—will bring you face-to-face with the enormously exciting cultural heritage you have as a user of English spelling. The English language itself is a glorious, infinitely useful, preposterously complex, endlessly fascinating tool that, like all languages, allows us to utilize to a wonderful extent one of the most basic by-products of being human—our expelled breath.

We can use this by-product to declare our love, call for help, recite a poem, discuss a work project with a colleague, ask for a bank loan, wish someone a happy birthday, and to do a myriad—indeed, an infinite variety—of other things.

But here's the problem: The English language, like all languages, starts to fade the instant it has been spoken. Within a fraction of a second the spoken sounds we heard have expired. Like Rose's lost lover Jack Dawson in the movie *Titanic*, spoken words can exist only in our memory or in the memories of the people who heard them spoken. Of course, it's true that due to technological developments during the past 130 years or so, spoken words can be recorded as sound on a recording medium, but the invention of sound recording is an extremely recent one by the standards of a completely different kind of recording technology that has existed for, most likely, about 10,000 years.

That other kind of recording technology is *writing*.

If spoken language can be written down, it can be remembered for as long as the writing medium continues to exist. Writing not only preserves language. It also—in a very real sense—cheats death.

This book is about a particular kind of death-cheating: the writing down, or the spelling, of the English language.

One reason why any kind of spelling, and especially the spelling of English, can be annoying is that we need to conform so much with authority—that is, with the accepted spelling standard—when we write. Even people who hate conforming with authority have to conform when they write, at least if they want to make themselves understood.

True, there are occasional exceptions. Some prominent players in subculture—some writers, for example, or pop groups—like to show how rebellious they are by indulging in misspellings. On the other hand, they might simply be trying to attract attention and win fame.

In the 1970s the British pop group Slade had a breakthrough hit with a song entitled (and cheekily spelled) "Cum on Feel the Noize." Slade became superstitious over the success of this song, and decided they needed to misspell the titles of all their songs if they wanted them to be successful. So the world was subsequently regaled with "Mama Weer All Crazee Now," "Coz I Luv You," "Look Wot Yu Dun," and "Gudby T'Jane." Fortunately, Slade came to their senses by the time they recorded and issued their most famous song, "Merry Christmas Everybody," which—outrageously—was spelled in the accepted fashion and enjoyed so much success Slade probably didn't bother wondering whether it would have done even better had they spelled the title "Meri Krismas Evrybodee."

There *is* something cheeky and subversive about misspellings, which is why many of us, and especially people who are young at heart or in body, like to use them in text messages or in e-mails. But no one really pretends these misspellings are anything other than precisely that: incorrectly written English. And even if the misspellings *do* somehow seem trendy and revolutionary, at least on first appearance, they really are nothing like as subversive as the *accepted* spellings, which have come into our writing system by a variety of ways that were, in their own day, trendy and outrageous.

There is plenty to say about English spelling, so let's get started. First, though, a few preliminary points.

Spellbound is designed to be a book for everyone, not only people with a professional (or masochistic) interest in English spelling. Because of this, I try to avoid using technical terms unless absolutely necessary. Such terms inevitably create a distance between a writer and reader that isn't particularly useful at the best of times, and especially not when one is writing about the technology of writing, which is first and foremost a communications technology and by its very nature designed to be accessible to the maximum number of users of a language.

I've also found it helpful to stick to the following rules:

- Modern English words quoted are enclosed in quotation marks as, for example, the word "misspell" here. This also applies to misspelled words, such as most of those written by my friend Nigel Molesworth, of whom more shortly.
- Words from foreign languages are italicized. I've also found it useful to employ italics for words quoted from Anglo-Saxon and Middle English. For English speakers, these languages are unfamiliar rather than foreign, but they are remote enough from modern English for some method of differentiation to be both useful and necessary.
- When I refer to sounds I *avoid* making use of the International Phonetic Alphabet (IPA), which is for specialists. Instead, I tend to refer to the sound of a given letter as, for example, "the *a*-sound" or "the *b*-sound." Where the sound needs to be identified with complete precision, I do this by referring to the sound in a particular context, such as "the *y*-sound in 'year.'"

The Bibliography at the back of *Spellbound* mentions the published sources I found most useful. I heartily recommend all of them as fascinating reading if you want to continue your exploration of the story of English spelling, perhaps the most improbable yet also somehow one of the most lovable stories ever told.

INTRODUCTION

Be a scribe! Put it in your heart
that your name should exist like theirs!...
A man has perished; his corpse is dust,
and his people have passed from the land;
It is a book which makes him remembered
in the mouth of a speaker.
More excellent is a [papyrus] roll than a built house,
than a chapel in the west.

> —From a poem, entitled by modern scholars
> *Eulogy to Dead Authors,* found on a papyrus
> manuscript, among the papyri of the author and
> scribe Qenherkhepshef at the tomb-chapels
> near Deir el-Medina, Egypt. The poem dates
> from the Nineteenth Dynasty (c. 1200 B.C.)

Writing, which preserves language, is really a form of magic. Why? Because by preserving language, it also preserves human thought. By doing this, it enables reason, emotion, and experience to overcome what would otherwise be the desperate and insurmountable barriers of forgetfulness and death. Make no mistake: That's magic, real magic. Spelling is a specialized form of writing that is simply the accepted way to write any writing system based substantially or entirely on an alphabet.

Writing is the best and, perhaps, the only *real* form of magic humans have ever possessed, or are ever likely to possess. Merlin, Houdini, the Wicked Witch of the West, Gandalf, Harry Potter, and any other wizard you may care to mention have never performed any magic that comes within a light-year of being half as magical as the technology of writing.

And writing is not only magical *in itself*. It also has the power to confer a kind of immortality on a writer, or on the person or thing being written about.

The verse above makes this point rather beautifully. The ancient Egyptian culture was—among many other things—an intensely materialistic one, yet here is a prominent scribe from their culture assuring us that writing is more important than anything else, because it can bring a scribe a kind of immortality, as indeed it brought to Qenherkhepshef himself. He bequeathed posterity much memorable poetry, and—remarkably for a writer who lived more than three millennia ago—extensive examples of his handwriting. His name may not be easy to spell, but it's now immortal.

Without writing, we would only have access to the thought from the past that had been expressed in spoken words, and remembered by generations of people who took care to retain these memories and passed them down from one generation to another. Would, in practice, many people bother to do this? It is, at best, doubtful. True, we are able to remember spoken words we have heard, we can even remember them for many decades. But ultimately these words will be forgotten when we die.

In Ray Bradbury's powerful novel *Fahrenheit 451*, first published in 1953, he describes a culture that has banned books and devotes much of its time to destroying them. The title of the novel refers to the temperature at which paper burns. A "fireman" in the story is not a man who puts fires out, but someone who deliberately *sets fire* to books.

In Bradbury's story, a group of subversives (by the standards of the prevailing society) takes painstaking efforts to memorize entire books so these works can be preserved for the future. Looking back with nostalgia to a past epoch when books were *not* routinely incinerated, one of their number observes:

> Books were only one type of receptacle where we stored a lot of things we were afraid we might forget... The magic is in what books say, how they stitched the patches of the universe together into one garment for us.

As well as being a form of real magic, writing is also a universally important invention; very likely the most important invention of all time.

Language itself is also an invention, of course. But language, while evidently something gradually evolved by humankind, is a very different kind of invention compared to writing. As far as we know, or can guess (and we can never be certain of this), language was probably never "invented" in any conscious sense at all.

Instead, it most likely evolved as certain primates gradually changed into hominids (manlike apes) and then subsequently into creatures that were our more recent ancestors. Our species, *Homo sapiens,* originated about 250,000 years ago. But paleontologists identify an earlier and later form of *Homo sapiens,* and estimate that it was only, in fact, about 100,000 years ago that our own, later form of *Homo sapiens* came into being.

We can't go back in time to find out whether our ancestors 100,000 years ago—or about 4,000 generations ago, which makes that prodigious gap of time seem slightly less daunting—were lucky enough to possess the blessing of spoken language. But it's very difficult indeed to believe that our ancestors, who were genetically identical to us, didn't have language. If they did, there's no particular reason to believe their languages weren't as sophisticated as ours are today. The languages of people living less technologically advanced lives than people in developed cultures are not any less sophisticated than the languages of those developed cultures. Linguists have proven this by analyzing the structures of known languages of the technologically unadvanced communities of the past and present. As the great linguist Edward Sapir observed in 1923, "When it comes to linguistic form, Plato walks with the Macedonian swineherd, Confucius with the headhunting savage of Assam."

So language most likely simply evolved. We don't know when language first came into being, but then neither do we know exactly when *we* first came into being. Very possibly our earlier hominid ancestors had *some kind* of language, and the most plausible and logical scenario seems to be that language evolved in subtlety and sophistication at much the same rate as we ourselves did.

Language and writing are very intimately linked. Writing, the great preserver of language, relies very heavily on language for its existence, though it doesn't necessarily rely *entirely* on language. Some signs—for example, the ones you find in airports—seem to have a direct meaning that bypasses language. These signs are surely a form of writing, for what else could they be? But they are exceptions. Otherwise, the synergy between language and writing is as dramatic and exciting as forked lightning. Indeed, there's even a well-documented case where writing has enabled a dead language to live again.

Hebrew, the language of the ancient Jewish people, was spoken until the third century B.C., when it gradually started to be replaced by the western dialect of the language known as Aramaic. This dialect of Aramaic was, for example, the mother tongue of Jesus Christ. Rent the video or DVD of Mel Gibson's *The Passion of the Christ* and you can hear Aramaic being spoken. By the time of Christ, Hebrew had died out as an everyday language. But it did survive in its written form, as the language of Jewish religious scripture and, to a certain extent, as a literary language.

Fast-forward nineteen centuries to the year 1880, when a Lithuanian Zionist named Eliezer Ben-Yehuda realized that Jewish people returning to Palestine required, as Ben-Yehuda elegantly put it, a "language in which we can conduct the business of life." Single-handedly, he began the massive task of building the Old Testament vocabulary of only 7,704 Hebrew words into a language that could be used for everyday purposes.

Scouring ancient Hebrew texts for old words and word-roots, Ben-Yehuda meticulously adapted them to fit modern meanings, inventing thousands of new Hebrew words in the process. Appropriately enough, the first new word he invented was *millon* ("dictionary"), because his life's work was the completion of the first four volumes of a seventeen-volume Hebrew lexicon. This lexicon was the foundation of the modern Hebrew language that is now, along with Arabic, the official language of modern Israel and the first language of about eighty percent of modern Israel's Jewish population.

Hebrew is the one known example of a dead language that has been revived into an everyday modern language. It is only written Hebrew that kept the language alive. Without writing, dead languages are forgotten once the last speaker of the language dies. Since the dawn of human language, untold numbers of languages must have been lost in this way. The revival of Hebrew is a case where a living language depended on writing for its very life.

Still, writing *is* clearly an invention, in the sense of be-

Allen County Public Library

ing a deliberate and artificially constructed tool or technology that allows us to achieve a certain desirable goal.

Writing was apparently invented by different people and in different cultures at different times. The main contenders for the invention of writing are the ancient Sumerians and the ancient Egyptians, both of whom had devised highly effective and comprehensive writing systems by about 3000 B.C. But there is evidence that writing systems existed in some parts of the world—including Central Europe—long before this, very likely as long ago as 8000 B.C. Of course, for all we know, writing might have been invented and then forgotten many times in the even more remote past.

The trouble is, we don't have enough information about the very earliest apparent attempts at writing to be certain they were comprehensive writing systems rather than comparatively simple systems of signs. For example, if you form a pair of twigs into the shape of an arrowhead to indicate to someone coming after you the direction you are proceeding in a forest, you are making use of a sign, and signs are indeed a kind of writing. But no one could really claim that your sign is writing in the sense that the written word "arrowhead" is writing.

What we do know is that from the very earliest days, the invention of writing *was* believed to be magical. For almost the entire length of time that writing has existed, writing was in all the countries of the world the preserve of an elite and privileged minority. Literacy, which in many countries is far from widespread even today, was justifiably regarded as something very special: a mark of education, status, even something to denote that the person possessing the ability to read and write played a key role in society. In ancient Sumeria and ancient Egypt, the inventors of writing were in fact priests. In ancient Egypt, it was priests and scribes who were the main readers and writers for more than a thousand years after writing was first invented.

It's not difficult to imagine why people who were able to make meaningful marks on wet clay or on papyrus—marks that crystallized and froze human thought for all time—should appear to others who *couldn't* do this to possess a magical skill. After all, writing does indeed cheat death, and what is more magical than that? In ancient Egypt, when notable people such as kings, queens, wealthy landowners, and merchants were buried, their sarcophagi were inscribed on the outside with hieroglyphic writing that included prayers to various deities for the safe conduct of the body as it passed into the shades beyond the world. Deceased ancient Egyptians were very literally bound with spells, which is what these written messages essentially were. When they died, ancient Egyptians were spellbound.

The idea that writing is basically a form of magic persists in some cultures. Even in developed countries today, people who haven't mastered reading and writing often treat writing with a particular awe. In other countries, people unused to writing may be astonished by it, or may indeed see it as a species of special magic. The writer

Karen Blixen, whose pseudonym was Isak Dinesen, recalls in her famous book *Out of Africa*, published in 1937, how the Kikuyu tribesmen she encountered reacted to their first exposure to writing:

> I learned that the effect of a piece of news was many times magnified when it was imparted by writing. The messages that would have been received with doubt and scorn if they had been given by word of mouth were now taken as gospel truth.

Not only taken as gospel truth, but also regarded as something momentous, fateful—even immortal. Magic this powerful was not, and is not, to be trifled with.

There's even a clear suggestion of the magical nature of writing in how the very word "spell" originated. "Spell" derives from the ancient Germanic word *spel*, meaning a "recital" or "tale." This word resulted in a word, also *spel*, that was part of the Old English or Anglo-Saxon language first spoken in about A.D. 500. The first and original meaning of the Old English *spel* was, following from the meaning of the ancient Germanic word, a "narrative" or "story."

Another meaning of "spell," first recorded in 1579, is still with us today; it means a special set of words, formulae, or verse possessing magical powers.

Where did the second, magical, meaning come from? We can't know for certain, but perhaps we can imagine how our ancestors, so dependent on spoken stories for their entertainment and their understanding of the world, might have started to see those who told the best stories as sages, and eventually even as magicians possessed of dark secrets.

The sense of "spell" meaning a narrative or story has left modern English, but you can still see a trace of it (English is a language with many old skeletons in its cupboard) in the modern word "gospel." Originally this was "good spell" or "good news." Which makes sense: The biblical gospels are, after all, accounts of the life of a man who gave us advice about how to enter heaven and who later came back from the dead. If you're a Christian, that will certainly be good news, and even if you're not, it sounds pretty magical.

By about A.D. 1300 the verb "to spell" had appeared, meaning the process of reading or writing a text letter by letter. This meaning came into English via an Old French word, *espeller*, which also originally derived from the ancient Germanic word *spel*.

The idea of spelling out a text letter by letter appears quite different from the meaning of the word *spel* as a recital or tale, but in fact there was a close connection. A tale will have its most potent effect only if all its elements—its letters, that is—are in the right order. The same is true, of course, of a magical formula.

Indeed, spelling was considerably *more* magical in the past, when far fewer people knew how to do it than is the case today. The literate elite enjoyed access to the written-down knowledge accumulated over the past, and so had the enormous privilege of being able to benefit from that knowledge, add to it, and pass it down to posterity—or at least to those whom they saw fit to bless with this knowledge. Magic is the art of producing extraordinary physical effects that defy logic. The elite who could read, write, and spell were—not unreasonably, perhaps—believed to be likely to possess magical powers.

The link between magic and writing occurs again and again in the story of writing—and also in this book. There is even a regular reminder of the link in popular culture. In the Harry Potter stories, for instance, when Harry, Hermione, and Ron want to seek out the oldest, darkest, and most magical secrets, they usually head for the Hogwarts library. An interesting additional point is that in some of the Harry Potter movies, the location for the Hogwarts library is the picturesque medieval Duke Humphrey library—completed in 1450—at the Bodleian Library in Oxford.

And besides, hasn't magical lore *always* ultimately been thought of as something that is written down? Deprived of their books of spells, wizards might even lose their power. Take a look, for example, at Shakespeare's play *The Tempest*. Toward the end, the wizard Prospero forecasts how he will give up magic once he has used it to achieve a reconciliation with his former enemies:

> *But this rough magic*
> *I here abjure: and, when I have required*
> *Some heavenly music,—which even now I do,—*

To work mine end upon their senses, that
This airy charm is for, I'll break my staff,
Bury it certain fathoms in the earth,
And deeper than did ever plummet sound
I'll drown my book.

The very notion of a holy book, such as the Christian Bible, the Muslim Koran, or the Jewish Talmud, stems from a time when most people couldn't read and write, when writers were frequently regarded as having magical powers and insight, and when the written-down wisdom of holy scripture was seen as having a divine inspiration, or even being written directly by God.

But we don't really need to contemplate magicians or books of spells to realize that writing is the most inspired and important invention people have ever devised. It's been very substantially responsible for our progress as a species from half-starved hunters and subsistence farmers to builders of cities and voyagers to the moon. Without the magic of writing, each new human generation would have little choice but to start understanding the world again more or less from scratch, rather than enjoying the infinitely valuable privilege of being able to enjoy and benefit from what has already been learned.

And if we are going to write, we had better write *accurately*. If we use an alphabetical writing system, as we do if we are writing English, we had better spell English properly. If we don't, we aren't—so to speak—going to get our magic right and our spells aren't going to work. And if our spells don't work, how can we possibly expect to make everything we can of our lives? How can we expect people we like to respect us? How can we expect people we love to love us back? How can we expect our customers to want to stay with us? How can we expect our boss to want to promote us?

Above all, if we don't spell properly, how can we possibly expect our lives to be magical?

Part One

—

Spelling in Action

Chapter 1

Method in the Madness?

"What's your name, sir?" enquired the judge.
"Sam Weller, my lord," replied that gentleman.
"Do you spell it with a 'V' or a 'W'?" enquired the
   judge.
"That depends upon the taste and fancy of the speller,
   my lord," replied Sam.

—Charles Dickens, *The Pickwick Papers* (1837)

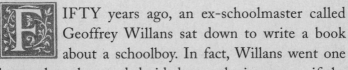IFTY years ago, an ex-schoolmaster called Geoffrey Willans sat down to write a book about a schoolboy. In fact, Willans went one better than that, and decided to make it seem as if the book were *written by* his schoolboy, Nigel Molesworth.

Nigel is one of English literature's great comic creations. He entices us to luxuriate in his anarchic, outrageous, yet curiously innocent world. From the moment he bursts into existence on the title page of *Down With Skool!*—the first of the four Molesworth books—Nigel reveals himself to be a keen observer of the foibles and cruelties of humanity.

The school he attends—St. Custard's—is run by a

ghoulish headmaster, Mr. GRIMES, whose surname is always written in uppercase by a terrified Nigel. GRIMES supplements his educational income by running an extracurricular whelk stall. We're reliably informed by Nigel that GRIMES would very gladly arrange for all the pupils to be driven off a cliff in a bus, were it not that this would deprive him of his livelihood.

The other masters are hardly an improvement. They include the alarmingly unpredictable Sigismund, the mad math master. There is also a considerate, narrow-eyed pedagogue who observes to one boy before caning him, "Your psychoanalyst may say one thing, Blatworthy, I say another. And my treatment is *free*." The masters, pupils, and parents provide a wide-ranging panorama of passions, appetites, and vices: There are few crevices of the human condition into which Nigel does not insert an inky finger.

One thing Nigel certainly can't do, though, is *spell*. In his world, masters are very "ferce" and go around brandishing "kanes." He also airs his opinion that "peotry" is "sissy stuff that rhymes" and informs us that a boy might learn that everything in Latin happened a long time ago, but only if he can stay awake in class for "long enuff." As for football (soccer), many professional—and national— teams of today might echo his sentiments on the matter . . .

Foopball is a tuough game but it is a pity you canot win by hacking everbode.

"Everybody," that is. Much of the fun of the Molesworth books is their cranky spelling, which one can't help feeling Geoffrey Willans knew all too well from his own days as a schoolmaster. Yet Nigel's spelling is never so erratic that it makes no sense at all; there is always plenty of method in the madness.

And after all, why *not* spell "canes" as "kanes"? Why *not* write "enuff" for "enough," especially when the sound "ough" in English can also be pronounced as in "cough," "plough," "borough," "dough," "nought," and even two ways in that town name non–English speakers find so intimidating: "Loughborough"? Doesn't spelling "enough" as "enuff" constitute a magnificent subversive revenge? Spell it that way, and the whole established world of orthodoxy, authority, law, repression, and edict—the sort of world which, incidentally, once led to small boys being caned by sadistic masters—starts to tremble.

Yet Nigel hasn't the slightest interest in starting a revolution in spelling, let alone a revolution in society. All he's doing is spelling words as if the way they *sound* is the way they should be spelled. "Enuff," for example, is obviously an incorrect spelling according to accepted rules. But if archaeologists from the distant future were to find a copy of *Down With Skool!* and see the spelling "enuff," they would gain a much better insight into how the word was pronounced from about A.D. 1500 onward than if they found a copy of *The Times* containing the correct spelling "enough." This, much less helpfully, reveals how the word was pronounced from about A.D. 900 to A.D. 1500. Nigel was inadvertently giving to posterity a *phonetic spelling*—that is, a spelling which sets down letters that aim as closely as possible to evoke the actual *sounds* of the spoken language.

Without phonetic spellings many of the great writing systems of the past would still be undeciphered. It is not known exactly how the vowel sounds of the classical Egyptian language of the pharaohs were pronounced, and this lack of knowledge would very likely have made it impossible for posterity to decipher Egyptian hieroglyphs, many of which were used to represent sounds just as our letters do (if not always consistently) in English. But fortunately for scholars, the hieroglyph writers were obliged to write Greek names such as "Ptolemy" and "Cleopatra" in hieroglyphs, and both the vowel and consonant sounds of *these* words were of course known. Scholars were able to use the hieroglyphic writing of these foreign names to offer a key to the sounds represented by a good range of hieroglyphs, and could then gradually build up an understanding of the sounds represented by other hieroglyphs from what was known of how classical Egyptian *consonants* were pronounced.

In her entertaining and informative bestseller *Eats, Shoots & Leaves*, Lynne Truss lovingly airs her annoyance with lazy and clumsy punctuation. Her indignation is abundantly justified, because incorrect punctuation can entirely change the meaning of a sentence. This might even have fatal consequences. For example, if you were mistakenly to punctuate the sentence "the old tiger approached its time to die" as "the old tiger approached; it's time to die," it would be *you* who would be dying, not the tiger. Getting punctuation right is essential if you want to make utterly clear what you mean.

But *spelling* is, on the whole, a rather different beast (so to speak). It's true that if you spell words incorrectly— which (in fact) means nothing more or less than "incorrectly according to what is regarded as acceptable within a particular country or culture"—you run the real risk of letting yourself down socially, professionally, and very possibly also financially. But it's also true that spelling *usually* does not need to be as precisely accurate as punctuation in order to convey an exact meaning. Put more simply, we can usually still understand words that are misspelled.

If we are spelling perfectionists like my friend Clair-Marie (of whom rather more soon) we might—for example—feel irritated to see, on a bulletin board, little cards proclaiming messages such as "cook requred," or "accomadation available," or to see a stereo system advertised as being in "excellant" condition, but unless we're being absurdly (and in fact dishonestly) pedantic we know what the advertisers *mean*. As the novelist Anthony Burgess pointed out in his superb book about language, *Language Made Plain,* a "guage" does its job just as efficiently as a "gauge," and "parrallel" lines still meet at infinity.

Indeed, even if words are *extremely* misspelled we can still read them, apparently because we tend to read—at least when we are fairly expert at reading—by focusing on the *entire image* of the word, and particularly on the first and last letters. If you don't believe this, try reading the following, which is the first paragraph of this chapter spelled in a different way:

Ftify yares ago, an ex-soochlmeatsr celald Geoffrey Willans sat dwon to wtire a book aubot a scoohlboy. In fcat, Willans wnet one beettr tahn taht, and dcdeied to make it seem as if the book wree *wttiren by* his scohol-boy, Nigel Molesworth.

In this passage, apart from the proper names, all the words longer than three letters have had their internal letters jumbled up (with the letters in word-compounds kept within the separate compounds), yet the paragraph presents no real difficulty to the native English speaker, or to anyone who has a good command of English as a second or foreign language. This example demonstrates that when we read familiar words we do assimilate and read them individually in their entirety rather than spell them out letter by letter.

Indeed, this point rather seems to be corroborated, not contradicted, by the fact that we have more difficulty reading a jumbled-up word, even if the first and last letters remain in the same position, when the other letters are in exactly the *reverse* order of what they should be. For example, "cetcidartnod" now reveals itself as much less readily readable than "contradicted." We do indeed appear to read whole words by their overall image, and are likely to become confused if the internal letters in a longish word are completely different from how they should be, rather than simply jumbled up a little.

But while we can usually make sense of misspelled words, the fact remains that spelling *does* matter. Of course it does. It matters enormously. The quality of your spelling will probably play a role in your career advancement, and even in the quality of your social life. We accept that most of us have words which we can't always spell accurately, but if you spell *really* badly, some people whose opinion you value may take you less seriously than you would like.

This is, in fact, distinctly unfair, because whichever way you look at it, the fact remains that the spelling of English is about as susceptible—at least superficially—to rational explanation as GRIMES's whelk stall is. Many people, whether native speakers of English or those learning English as a second language, regard English spelling as at best a joke and at worst a nightmare deliberately designed to bamboozle and perplex anyone who tries to learn it.

As users of an alphabetic writing system, we are aware that English spelling basically aims to equate letters in a word with the sounds of our spoken language. But how efficiently and consistently does English do this? The answer is, pretty *inefficiently* and *inconsistently*.

If you can write in an alphabetic language other than English you'll probably have noticed that the link between the sounds of the spoken words in that language and the letters on the page are somehow much more direct and regular than when you write English.

The Italian word *forse*, for example, meaning "perhaps," is pronounced simply by saying every sound in order. In Italian it sounds like "for-seh," not like "force," which is probably how the word would be pronounced if it existed in English.

The Latin word *fortasse*, from which *forse* derived, was also—as far as is known—pronounced by every letter's sound being spoken. In English we are so used to letters being silent that our instinct as English speakers would probably be to pronounce *fortasse* as something like "fortass."

Take a more obscure European language, Finnish. While English, Italian, and Latin are, despite all their differences, members of the same Indo-European language family, Finnish is a member of a completely different language family, Finno-Ugrian, which is why Finnish words often look so unfamiliar. (For example, "I love you. Do you understand? I love you" is *Minä rakastan sinua. Ymmärrätko? Minä rakastan sinua*, which is quite a mouthful on Saturday night or even Sunday morning.) But Finnish words are spelled more consistently than English words in that the written sounds correspond in a very regular way to spoken sounds. Finnish words may look strange, but they're easy to pronounce because you just say every sound in order, even to the extent of repeating the sound of a consonant if it is a double consonant. So, for example, the word *kyllä*, meaning "yes," is pronounced something like "cool-lah" while *kylä*, meaning "village," is pronounced something like "coo-lah" with only one *l*-sound in the middle. Pronouncing written Finnish is in fact a piece of cake, or *kakku*, which is spoken something like "kak-koo."

The word "phonetic" is a convenient word to describe a link between a sound and a letter. A language that is highly phonetic is one where the same letter invariably represents the same sound. A language becomes less phonetic the less this is so. A strong case could be made for regarding English as one of the least phonetic alphabetic languages—perhaps even *the* least phonetic—on the planet. There are so many examples of inconsistencies— even outrageous inconsistencies—in English spelling that it is almost unnecessary to provide examples. But some examples of the many respects in which English is illogical ought to drive the point home:

◆ Different sounds are frequently represented by the same letter, or combinations of letters. A revealing example of this is the spectrum of notorious words "cough," "enough," "borough," "nought," "plough," and—yes—"Loughborough," the unassuming town I've already mentioned, which is just north of Leicester in the English Midlands. And think of "bite"/"night," "taught"/"thought," "bait"/"gate." There are thousands of other examples. One consequence of the fact that the same sounds in English are frequently spelled in different ways is that it is perfectly possible to construct nonsensical spellings that are entirely logical when you look at how the sounds are used in other words. For example, the writer George Bernard Shaw once pointed out that we are entitled to spell the word "fish" as "ghoti," using the *gh* spelling from "cough," the *o* spelling from "women," and the *ti* from "nation." And do you know a girl called *Eaufaeleyu*? This is simply "Ophelia," with the *eau* in "plateau," the *f* in "field," the *ae* in "Caesar," the *l* in "lip," the *ey* in "key," and the *u* in "but."

• The same sounds in English are frequently represented by a different letter or combination of letters. Many of these words are *homophones*—words that sound the same but have different meanings; for instance, "gate"/"gait," "made"/"maid," "mettle"/"metal," "tea"/"tee." There are in fact thousands of homophones in English because most one-syllable English nouns double as noun and verb, e.g., "cook"/"cook," "knife"/"knife," "nail"/"nail," "right" in the senses of "right and left" and "to right a wrong." However, *these* homophones are spelled in the same way, because the verb is derived from the noun, or vice versa. The very fact that homophones can be spelled in different ways shows just how inconsistent English spelling really is.

• English spelling contains numerous words that feature silent letters. Indeed, this is a notorious aspect of the English spelling system and causes great difficulty to anyone trying to learn how to spell and read English. Just a few of the many examples: "debt," "island," "knee," "knight," "scissors." The problem is hardly helped when the word containing the silent letter is also a homophone with another word of unrelated meaning, as is the case with words such as "knight"/"night."

• The use of the letter *e*—the most common letter in

written English—is hugely inconsistent. It is often not pronounced at all, and seems practically redundant, as in words such as "image," "imagine," and "submerge." The letter *e* may, rather more usefully, reflect a change in the vowel sound of the spelled word to distinguish it from another word that does not have the final *e*. Examples are: "car"/"care," "jut"/"jute," "mad"/"made." I can still remember being taught at school, at the age of seven or thereabouts, to read words such as "made" and "rode" by thinking of the *e* as "magical," because it changed the sound of the letter that was two letters behind it into the *name* of the letter—that is, "mad" becomes "made" and "rod" turns into "rode." A friend who teaches at a primary school recently told me she finds the notion of the *e* being magical a useful teaching aid even today.

◆ Generally, written letters in English can stand for a wide—even alarming—range of sounds. Consider, to take just one example, the different sounds represented by the written letter *o* in the following five words: "police," "Oswald," "ozone," "nation," and "zoo." Or consider how written letters can represent a range of different sounds in English in the numerous ways the *ee*-sound is written down in all the following words: "Caesar," "conceive," "fee," "field," "key," "machine," "me," "people," "quay," "sea," "subpoena." Similarly, the *sh*-sound is written down in a range of different ways: "chaperone," "conscious," "eschew," "fuchsia," "fissure," "mansion," "mission," "nation," "nauseous," "ocean," "shoe," "sugar," "suspicion." You don't even need to seek out longer words to see just how inconsistent

English spelling is. Consider, for example, the problems of spelling "to," "too," and "two."

In all fairness to English spelling, there *are* a few instances where spelling has a helpful logicality and assists with understanding a word's meaning. For example, the English past tense is generally represented by the final letters *ed,* even though the past tense ending can actually be pronounced in three different ways, as in the words "liked," "loved," and "waited." The English plural is also usefully represented by the letter *s,* which covers the three different plural sounds we use, as in the words "cakes," "boys," and "daisies." Another small benefit of English spelling is that we don't use modifying marks to letters, such as the accented *é* and *è* of modern French or the umlaut of German for letters such as *ä* and *ö*. But in general, logic in English spelling is about as rare as a joke in a dictionary.

This basic illogicality of English spelling is bad enough as far as any attempt to master it is concerned. But an even worse difficulty—and this is the real problem we have to confront when we learn to read and write English—is that English spelling is, on the face of it, extremely *arbitrary.* I use the word "arbitrary" here in the sense of implying that there is no particular reason for something to be the way it is, other than that the way it is *is* the way it is.

In English spelling, the main consequence of this arbitrariness is that in the vast majority of cases we simply have to learn how to spell a word by learning how to spell it. There *are* some rules that may help us to spell better, but generally these rules apply only to a very small number of words.

As Vivian Cook points out in his amusing book about spelling, *Accomodating Brocolli in the Cemetary*, the famous rule "*i* before *e* except after *c*" is all very well, but it doesn't cover many words. In fact, it covers only about twenty words in all. These words are hardly a very substantial part of the vocabulary of an English speaker, for whom a typical average vocabulary is reckoned to be about 10,000 words.

In practice, apart perhaps from the well-known but not especially useful rule just quoted, it's probably easier to learn individual spellings than to learn what rules there are for spelling. Obviously some illogical but common patterns of how sounds are represented in spelling *do* emerge—for example, "ph" to represent the Greek-derived *f*-sound in words such as "photograph," "pharaoh," "phosphate," and "graphite"—but generally there are few simple but effective rules to guide us in how we should spell English.

Yet... despite the apparent illogicality of most English spellings, there *is* in fact often an abundance of method in the madness. Indeed, one of my main reasons for writing *Spellbound* is that many English spellings which seem at first sight purely arbitrary can, in fact, be very well explained *by focusing on the story of the spelling in question*.

This story of the spelling is, as we might expect, usually related to the story of the word itself. Take the three words

Vivian Cook uses in the title of his book, which are of course deliberately misspelled for facetious effect.

I blithely write "of course" here, but I had better be honest and confess that the word "accommodation" was, until about ten years ago (I am forty-nine now), always a bit of a spelling bugbear for me. Like many people I used to spell it with just one *m*. I also had a problem with "similar" (which I used to write as "similiar") and "liaise" (I have often misspelled this as "liase"). Incidentally, for the avoidance of any possible doubt, the correct spelling of "misspelled" is "misspelled," and while (according to the *Oxford English Dictionary*) "misspelt" and "misspelled" are both acceptable, "misspelt" is more usual in British English and "misspelled" in American English. So, make sure you spell "misspell" correctly and don't misspell "misspell" as "mispell," "mis-spell," or "miss-spell," nor misspell "misspelled" as "mispelled," "mis-spelled," or "miss-spelled."

No one could really deny that "accomodating" is on the face of it a perfectly reasonable spelling; it is just that according to our arbitrary spelling standard, you need a double "m" in the middle. Similarly, "brocolli" and "cemetary" are misspelled words that convey the meaning of the word perfectly adequately; it's just that they are not correctly spelled according to the same arbitrary standard that applies to "accommodating."

In fact, if we look at the origins of the words "accommodating" and "broccoli," we find that their correct spellings derive very directly from the original foreign words that were borrowed from other languages. "Accommodation," first recorded in English in the mid–sixteenth century, stems from the past participle of the Latin word *accommodare,* meaning "to fit." "Broccoli," which came into the English language about a century after "accommodation," derives from the plural form of the Italian word *broccolo,* meaning "cabbage sprout or head." (The late Cubby Broccoli, the producer of the James Bond movies, derived his surname from the fact that his forebears were farmers who ingeniously produced broccoli by crossing an Italian vegetable known as rabe with a cauliflower. The result shook, rather than stirred, the world's vegetable markets.) "Cemetery" comes from the Latin word *coemeterium,* which stems from the ancient Greek word *koimeterion,* meaning "dormitory." Meanings of words always change over time. Incidentally, it was usual until the mid–eighteenth century to spell "cemetery" as "coemeterion," which obviously more precisely preserves the original spelling of the Latin word.

You'll see from these three examples that their modern English spelling is based closely on the foreign words from which they are derived. This process is very typical of English spelling. We can readily formulate a rule, that "for words borrowed from other languages, English spelling tends to a large degree to preserve the original spelling of the borrowed word." The word may be made more "English," for instance by modifying the ending, but it derives closely from the original spelling.

Why is English so willing to retain the original spelling of foreign words it borrows? Some languages—Norwegian, for example—go much further than English does in adapting the spelling of borrowings to their own spelling conventions. Norwegian is, in fact, very much *unlike* English in how it deals with foreign words when it borrows them, as it only feels "comfortable" with a foreign word after it has "Norwegianized" it. When Norwegian borrowed "mayonnaise" from French via English, it spelled the word *majones*. In much the same way, the English words "strike" and "service" have been borrowed by Norwegian and rendered as, respectively, *streik* and *sørvis*. The letter *ø* in Norwegian is pronounced rather like the "-er" in the word "service" itself.

Professor Stephen Walton, a British cultural historian who has taught himself Norwegian to a bilingual level and runs a language institute in Norway, says he believes Norwegian tends to nativize borrowed foreign words essentially for political reasons. "Norway prides itself on being a highly egalitarian society," he told me. "Norwegians regard adapting foreign word-borrowings into the style of their own language as a democratic thing to do."

Which is a fair point, perhaps. After all, there *is* sometimes something a trifle elitist about the way some English speakers keep foreign words—especially French ones—very much intact. It's like the old joke about the pseudointellectual who, having been accused of being pretentious, indignantly replies, "Pretentious, *moi?*"

In many languages other than English, the pronunciation of the borrowings may be recognizably similar to the original but the spelling may look strikingly different from the spelling of the borrowed word. For example, the Finnish word *kahvi* is a borrowing from English "coffee," but spelled (and also pronounced) according to Finnish sound conventions, which include a prohibition on the *f*-sound in native Finnish words. Similarly, Japanese words have been borrowed from English since Japan opened up to foreign trade in the mid–nineteenth century. Borrowings include *biru* for beer, *takeshi* for taxi, and *hoteru* for hotel, though the situation here is complicated by the fact that these are phonetic spellings as Japanese does not use the Roman alphabet.

Generally, languages like Finnish that have fairly regular and "logical" spelling systems are more likely to create a new spelling for a borrowing in order to make the borrowing seem more familiar and to fit in with the language's sound patterns; patterns that are recorded very consistently in the way the language is written down. Such languages differ in this respect from English, which has so little regularity in its spelling that the borrowed foreign word may as well be spelled much as it was spelled in its original form.

Indeed, English makes particularly heavy use of borrowed foreign words, so that another few words whose spelling resembles the language from which the word originated are not likely to look out of place, any more than another few pieces of old junk are likely to look out of place in a junk shop.

There's a practical point to consider, too. Because English spelling is so fundamentally illogical, if we did want to adapt the spellings of foreign words to the English style, *it would be difficult to know how best to do it.* The reason is that there is not, in fact, a suitable English style for spelling foreign words. And even if there were, there would hardly be any point in using it because the language as a whole would still have masses of irregularity of spelling. It would be like trying to cool down an erupting volcano by tossing a bucketful of water onto it.

Another important factor is that the English language is extremely tolerant of retaining foreign word-forms in the first place. Not all languages are.

Sometimes this intolerance is due to political factors. For example, in the highly (and, as things turned out, disastrously) nationalistic Germany of the 1930s, there was a strong feeling that foreign words should not be used in the German language. And so, when television was invented and brought into service in the 1930s, a German word for "television" was needed. The specially created word, *Fernsehgerät,* means, literally, "far-seeing equipment," although today a more simplified version *Fernsehen* ("far-seeing") is more common. The rather sinister-sounding *Fernsehgerät* was perhaps appropriate for a machine that would so often show Adolf Hitler addressing adoring and deluded crowds. But in more recent decades Germany has become less chauvinistic in this respect. The German word for "computer," for example, is simply *Computer*.

Even today, for some languages, the question of whether or not to borrow a foreign spelling doesn't actually arise because speakers of those languages prefer to create their own version of a foreign word. They may do this less for political reasons than because either the borrowed word sounds too alien to the language borrowing it, or the speakers prefer to create a word of their own that uses familiar elements of meaning.

Take Finnish, for example. The Finnish language has a fairly simple "vowel + consonant" syllable system (as does Japanese; some linguists believe there is a very remote connection) and doesn't like consonant clusterings in the same syllable. When 1980s Britain was ruled by the Iron Lady, the name "Thatcher" was a nightmare for Finnish people to pronounce (just as it was for Mrs. Thatcher's political opponents). The closest most Finns got to saying the name was something that sounded a bit like "tat-yer." Because words borrowed from English and other languages would usually sound too alien in Finnish, and because in any case the Finns feel happier with words that utilize Finnish meaning-elements, the language usually prefers to make up its own words. So, for example, in Finnish the word "computer" is *tietokone* or "knowledge machine." And because Finnish pronounces every vowel rather than running vowels and consonants together into a single sound as we often do in English, the word *tietokone* is actually pronounced something like "tee-eh-toh-ko-ne."

"Telephone" in Finnish is *puhelin*, or "speaking machine," while "airplane" is *lentokone*, which literally means "flying machine," a phrase that was actually used in English in the early part of the twentieth century. In colloquial Finnish *lentokone* is usually shortened to *kone*—meaning "machine." At airports they use this abbreviation when announcing that planes have landed, so that they say things like "the machine from New York to Helsinki has landed," rather as if The Terminator had just flown in.

In fact, when the telephone was first invented in the late nineteenth century, it was originally called *telefoni* by the Finns, but in 1897 the word *puhelin* was suggested in a Finnish newspaper, and the word soon caught on.

There is another northern European language that indulges in even more imaginative flights of fancy with coined words than Finnish does. This is Icelandic, a member of the North Germanic language family. It is in fact a language that preserves many features of the original Viking language, Old Norse. It is said that a Viking visiting modern Iceland could make a lot of sense out of a newspaper written in Icelandic.

The Icelandic people have found quite a few fun ways to adopt modern words—especially relating to technology—into their ancient language. Being justly proud of their language, Icelanders have cultural reasons for this. They actually have a national committee that protects the integrity of their language, and has even been known to hold a competition to decide how a necessary new word should be translated into Icelandic. So, for example, as a result of one of these competitions, the Icelandic word for "computer" is *tölva*, which ingeniously derives from the words *tala*, meaning "number" (and is connected via Norman French with the English word "tally"), and *völva*, meaning "prophetess." The word "computer" in Icelandic therefore means, literally, "number prophetess." Maybe Bill Gates should know this.

It gets better. In Icelandic, "television" is *sjónvarp*, which means "picture-thrower." Awesome! But my favorite coined word in Icelandic is *friðþjófur* (yes, really) in which the letter *ð* is pronounced like the "th" in "the" and *þ* like "th" in "thin." This word *friðþjófur* means, literally, "thief of the peace," and is used to refer to the pager, that device worn by people who are on call, and also by people who aren't on call but who want to look as if they are.

English, on the other hand, is not only *happy* to borrow foreign words intact, but does so with considerable enthusiasm. The number of borrowings in English from other languages is enormous; indeed, the breadth of the borrowings makes English an exceptionally rich language, at least as far as range of vocabulary is concerned. As a matter of practical fact, English probably has more words—in excess of 100,000, including technical terms—than any other language in the world, and many thousands of them are borrowings from other languages. The borrowings reflect the extent to which English-speaking people have, now as in the past, come into contact with numerous foreign cultures and have also been more than happy to assimilate aspects of the foreign culture (and, a cynic might add, on occasion appoint themselves rulers of it).

Here are just a few of the words English has borrowed from foreign languages over the past few centuries and made its own, often to the extent that we might find ourselves surprised that such a familiar "English" word had such an exotic origin:

ITALIAN

Music: *allegro, andante, crescendo, diminuendo, legato, obbligato, pizzicato, staccato, vibrato*

Food and drink: *cappuccino, latte, pizza*

Architecture: *corridor, cupola, grotto, pedestal, pergola, piazza, rotunda*

Literature: *burlesque, canto, extravaganza, stanza*

A word whose precise origins are uncertain but which probably also comes from Italian is the word "ghetto." This appears to derive either from the Italian word *borgetto*, a diminutive form of *borgo* meaning "borough," or from the word *getto* meaning "foundry"—because the world's first ghetto (that is, a part of a city where Jews were obliged to live), which was formed in Venice in 1516, was sited near an iron foundry. Italian ghettos were relatively humane, and were designed more to house the Jewish community than to oppress Jewish people. It is only in more recent decades, due to historical events that are only too well known, that the word "ghetto" has acquired the unpleasant connotation it has today.

SPANISH
armada, cannibal, cigar, galleon, guerrilla, matador, mosquito, orange, tornado, vanilla

"Potato" (often misspelled with an extra *e*, as it once memorably was by the former U.S. Vice President Dan Quayle) and "tomato" have also come into English from Spanish, but were themselves borrowings from languages spoken by indigenous people in South American countries taken over by Spain. An interesting example of a borrowing with a subtle change of meaning is the word "bonanza." This word, derived from the Latin *bonus,* meaning "good," came into British English via American English in the early nineteenth century. Meaning "goodness" in Spanish, it was originally borrowed by English to mean "fair weather," but was used by miners in the United States to mean "prosperity." It was from this meaning that the modern English meaning of "spectacular windfall" soon developed.

ARABIC
alchemy, alcohol, algebra, alkali, almanac, arsenal, cipher, elixir, mosque, sugar, syrup, zenith, zero

HEBREW
amen, cherub, kibbutz, manna, messiah, pharisee, rabbi, sab-bath

Other Hebrew words commonly used in English are "hallelujah"—meaning "praise" and taken from the second-person plural imperative of the Hebrew verb *hallel*, "to praise"—and "kosher," which has come to mean in modern English not just food that is prepared according to Jewish law but also, more broadly, anything that is correct, genuine, and legitimate.

WELSH
flannel

CORNISH
This language died out in Cornwall as a mother tongue in the eighteenth century. However, it still lives in English in the word for a seabird, "gull," which is a borrowing from the Cornish word *gullan*.

GAELIC AND IRISH
blarney, bog, brogue, galore, hooligan, leprechaun, shamrock, slogan, Tory, whisky

NORWEGIAN
ombudsman, ski

FINNISH
sauna

RUSSIAN
*kvass, mammoth, ruble, samovar, sputnik, tsar, tundra, vodka
  (of course)*

The word "intelligentsia" is a complex borrowing. English has borrowed it from Russian, which borrowed it from Polish, which borrowed it from Latin.

CZECH
robot

HUNGARIAN
goulash, paprika

PORTUGUESE
dodo, flamingo, marmalade, molasses, port (wine), veranda

BASQUE
bizarre

TURKISH
caviar, coffee, fez, kiosk, turban

URDU
cushy

HINDI
cheetah, guru, jungle, loot, maharajah, mahatma, pajamas, punch (the drink), sahib, shampoo, thug

The word "juggernaut" comes from a title for the deity Krishna, a large model of whom is carried on an enormous cart at an annual festival in the Indian coastal town of Puri. In the past, many pious devotees were said to have thrown themselves in religious fervor under the cart, often crushing themselves to death.

PERSIAN
bazaar, caravan, chess, divan, khaki, paradise, shah, shawl

TAMIL
catamaran, curry

CHINESE
kowtow, sampan, tea, typhoon

JAPANESE
hara-kiri, judo, karaoke, karate, kimono, samurai, shogun, tycoon

MALAY
bamboo, ketchup

The word "junk" meaning a type of boat also comes from Malay, but the origin of "junk" meaning "rubbish" is unknown. "Orangutan" is from the Malay *orang hutan*, meaning "forest person."

POLYNESIAN
taboo, tattoo

AFRICAN LANGUAGES
chimpanzee, voodoo

The term "mumbo jumbo" comes from a word, spelled almost identically, for a grotesque idol said to have been worshiped in the past by various peoples from west Africa.

INUIT (ESKIMO)
anorak, kayak

"Igloo" is from the original word *iglu*, meaning "house."

ABORIGINAL AUSTRALIAN
boomerang, kangaroo, wallaby, wombat

I haven't listed here borrowings from Romance languages (including Latin and all historical forms of French) nor words that are a consequence of the legacy of English being a Germanic language. Romance borrowings are so extensive that it is no exaggeration to regard English as a hybrid of Romance and Germanic forms of language. This fact has enormous implications for English spelling, and—as we shall see—introduces much method into the apparent madness of English spelling.

The borrowings from the various foreign languages listed above are, in the main, ones that have come into the language over the past two centuries, an exceptionally rich period for the English language as far as borrowings from foreign languages are concerned. Many of these borrowings have been associated with the British Empire, which brought the British into intimate contact with foreign cultures. While often viewed with a certain contempt by British expatriates (the writer George Orwell once observed that the instant the British become truly aware of a foreign country, they invent a contemptuous term for its inhabitants), these cultures were energetically plundered for loanwords as well as for treasure.

With a few exceptions, in the list above I haven't given the original spellings of the words from which the English form was borrowed, because often the spelling of the original foreign word was not standardized anyway, and of course some of the languages are not written in the same alphabet as we use for English. But generally, the principle that English retains the spelling of foreign loanwords remains remarkably reliable.

And this principle has also applied throughout the 1,500-year evolution of the English language. The result? English spelling, today, is a fascinating, ragtag collection of words that have come into the language from many different sources and at many different times. And, for reasons we've seen, the spellings by and large retain the original spelling of the words from which the borrowings derived.

Rather than ridiculing English spelling, or resigning ourselves to regarding it as a nightmare, it's more useful—and in fact also more *true*—to see English spelling as something like a vast family of children that came from all over the world and have been lovingly fostered and nurtured into the adults we are likely to meet anytime we choose to write the words that represent these "members of the family."

Alternatively, we might think of English as an enormous cupboard in which we keep curiosities that we have been gathering for fifteen centuries. We may worry that our collection of curiosities has rather outgrown the cupboard; we may feel alarmed, when we carefully prize open the door, that we will never know what is likely to come tumbling out, but we would hardly be likely to view our collection with anything other than a mixture of awe and affection.

Indeed, you might as well *enjoy* your vast family of grown-up foster children, whose origins may date from last week or from around A.D. 500. Because, like it or not, you don't have any real choice about the way English is spelled any more than you do about what the words of spoken English actually *are*. In later chapters we give some thought to the bold attempts that have been made (and not only recently, either) to reform English spelling. But with the exception of a few words whose spelling has indeed been successfully reformed, and also with the exception of the really only very limited spelling differences between American English and British English, the efforts of these reformers have come to little or nothing. They have turned out to have as little effect on the onward progression of the vast, weighty, proud juggernaut that is English spelling as the brave martyrs who threw themselves under the wheels of the original juggernaut.

While I was gathering material for this book, I happened to visit a branch of a popular Scottish-sounding fast-food chain in the town of Sittingbourne in Kent, England. It was a summer's day, but wet—the sort of day when even if you don't regret going out without an umbrella at first, you will later. I took refuge from the drizzle by partaking of the three major food groups of burger, fries, and soft drink. As I carried them to a table, I noticed the following sign at the foot of a staircase leading up to the first floor. This is not, by the way, a story writers invent to put in books like this; this really happened. And I'm quoting the words exactly as they were on the sign:

> Top lobby
> closed due to leeks
> in the roof
> because of weather

Until the moment I saw this sign, I'd honestly never guessed that warm, wet weather can lead to a substantial crop of leeks growing on the upper floors of buildings. Nor had I known that these hostile vegetables—rather like the deadly, ambulatory plants in John Wyndham's science-fiction horror story *The Day of the Triffids*—could be so dangerous and numerous it would be unwise to allow anybody to approach them. Still, what do you expect from the only vegetable whose name contains "eek"! Broccoli would be *so* much friendlier.

Fortunately, it's only rarely that leeks grow in such abundance as to be so risky to approach, but poor spelling remains a hazard for all of us, and not only for the damage it might inflict on our job prospects, either.

I have a friend called Clair-Marie who is exceptionally beautiful, charming, and switched-on, and as a natural consequence much wooed by young men. Unfortunately for them, she's also an absolute stickler for adherence to conventions of spelling and punctuation. Nothing irritates her more than someone who makes spelling mistakes.

Not long ago an optimistic young swain conceived a grand passion for Clair-Marie. He started besieging her (though he would have probably spelled it "beseiging" or even "beseeging") with e-mails and text messages. Unfortunately, these were riddled with spelling and punctuation errors, and what little ardor Clair-Marie had had for the poor chap in the first place soon evaporated. "Eventually I had to ask him to stop e-mailing me," she explained to me. "I didn't mean to be horrible to him, but the horrible spelling in his e-mails was putting me in a bad mood for the rest of the day."

I thought she might have been joking, but she wasn't.

Before Clair-Marie delivered her draconian prohibition, she did at least contemplate the possibility of becoming involved with her suitor, but the more of his e-mails she read the more she doubted she could ever care for someone who spelled so badly.

While I thought this particular young man was most likely a lost cause, I did suggest to Clair-Marie that in the future when she met someone who at least had the potential to be Mr. Right (but not Mr. Write), she could explain at the outset how important accurate spelling was to her. I told her I thought she could even link incremental romantic advances to the spellings of increasingly difficult to spell words.

"The next person who wants to win your affection," I suggested, "ought to be prepared to improve his spelling in order to do it."

She asked me what exactly I meant, so I proposed a list of stages of romantic progress with her and the words a suitor would have to spell in order to achieve them. She said she thought I was being ridiculous, but on reflection something like the following might not be a bad idea.

Stage of romantic progress	What you need to be able to spell to reach this stage
A quick kiss	BREVITY
A long kiss	PROTRACTED

A kiss on a sofa	OSCULATORY
Holding hands	AMBULATORY
A weekend together	IMPASSIONED
A week together	INEXHAUSTIBLE
A lifetime together	PHILOPROGENITIVE

In any event, being able to spell isn't only likely to be important in your work life. It might, just might, matter in your personal life, too. Oh, and it may also make you some money, especially if you happen to be a school pupil.

The National Spelling Bee was launched in 1925 by the *Courier-Journal* newspaper of Louisville, Kentucky. The meaning of the word "bee" in this sense means a gathering for work or amusement or to pursue a specific activity. The Spelling Bee, aimed at schoolchildren, was devised to feature a series of competitions, cash prizes, and a trip to the nation's capital. The idea was to stimulate interest among pupils in a subject that was normally considered dull and to give studious children the opportunity to become celebrities. In 1941 the Scripps Howard News Service took over the Spelling Bee and has run it ever since.

Today the Spelling Bee is a major competition in the United States, with the number of national finalists (from whom the winner is selected by vigorous competition) having grown over the years from just nine in 1925 to 274 in 2005. The first prize in the 2006 Bee was a total of $45,000 in cash plus a variety of other valuable prizes.

Here are the final words from each year that the winning contestants had to be able to spell in order to become national champions. (Note that there was no Spelling Bee in the years 1943 to 1945 due to the Second World War.)

1925	gladiolus	1952	vignette
1926	abrogate	1953	soubrette
1927	luxuriance	1954	transept
1928	albumen	1955	crustaceology
1929	asceticism	1956	condominium
1930	fracas	1957	schappe
1931	foulard	1958	syllepsis
1932	knack	1959	catamaran
1933	torsion	1960	troche
1934	deteriorating	1961	smaragdine
1935	intelligible	1962	esquamulose
1936	interning	1963	equipage
1937	promiscuous	1964	sycophant
1938	sanitarium	1965	eczema
1939	canonical	1966	ratoon
1940	therapy	1967	chihuahua
1941	initials	1968	abalone
1942	sacrilegious	1969	interlocutory
1946	semaphore	1970	croissant
1947	chlorophyl	1971	shalloon
1948	psychiatry	1972	macerate
1949	dulcimer	1973	vouchsafe
1950	meticulosity	1974	hydrophyte
1951	insouciant	1975	incisor

1976	*narcolepsy*	1992	*lyceum*
1977	*cambist*	1993	*kamikaze*
1978	*deification*	1994	*antediluvian*
1979	*maculature*	1995	*xanthosis*
1980	*elucubrate*	1996	*vivisepulture*
1981	*sarcophagus*	1997	*euonym*
1982	*psoriasis*	1998	*chiaroscurist*
1983	*Purim*	1999	*logorrhea*
1984	*luge*	2000	*demarche*
1985	*milieu*	2001	*succedaneum*
1986	*odontalgia*	2002	*prospicience*
1987	*staphylococci*	2003	*pococurante*
1988	*elegiacal*	2004	*autochthonous*
1989	*spoliator*	2005	*appoggiatura*
1990	*fibranne*	2006	*ursprache*
1991	*antipyretic*		

The National Spelling Bee is fun, and promotes good spelling around the United States. It also gives young people who may not be particularly good at sports a chance to shine and become national stars. But when all is said and done, the words you need to be able to spell to win the Bee are not exactly ones you'll need to use every day, or even once in a lifetime.

Besides, the enormous difficulty of the words that the winners of the National Spelling Bee have had to spell raises some very natural questions that we could very usefully consider before moving on to look at where exactly English spelling came from.

Why should we write a particular word in that particular way? Who *says* the word needs to be spelled like that? And, for that matter, why does writing need to be a system we have to learn in the first place? *Why can't we just do our own thing?*

Chapter 2

Visible Thought

The world was once all miracle. Then everything started to be explained. Everything will be explained in time. It's only a matter of waiting.

—Anthony Burgess, *Earthly Powers* (1980)

ANY people have dreamed, over the past few centuries, of creating a special kind of Holy Grail: a *universal* writing system that wouldn't need to be learned at all, and could be independent of language and culture, even of time.

It's a reasonable dream, if you think about it. After all, we can all make a stab at *drawing* things even if we don't have much, or any, innate talent for drawing. I am probably one of the worst drawers who has ever lived, but even I could (I think) draw a cat that looked enough like one for you to recognize what it was. If we all have some inherent ability to draw, why shouldn't we also have some innate ability to *write*?

In fact, there have been various attempts in the past to develop a workable, practical writing system that wouldn't need to be consciously *learned* at all, but which anyone could use merely by applying basic common sense. Recently, a brave attempt to achieve this ambition was made by the linguist and scholar Geoffrey Sampson, in his readable and thought-provoking book *Writing Systems*.

In the book, Sampson tries to write just one sentence in a "universal way," that is, in a way that *anybody* ought to be able to understand using basic common sense. If you can write one sentence in this way it's a fair bet you could write as many sentences as you wanted to write, so the "test sentence" is pretty crucial.

Sampson uses a sequence of little drawings, including a cat, a pointing finger, legs, and a mat to say: "The cat walked over the mat." Here is what he writes in order to try to convey this meaning in a universal way:

This is certainly a bold and brave attempt to achieve a difficult objective. Using the pointing finger to convey the idea of *the specific thing in question* (and so to translate the word "the") is ingenious, as is the use of the legs to show the idea of *walking*. The use of the clock and arrow to show the idea of the past is pretty obscure, though, as is the notion of "over" shown with the arrow above the rectangle.

For all Sampson's ingenuity, and even if you correctly

guessed what the "universal" sentence is supposed to mean, would it *really* be comprehensible to anybody in the world?

This is pretty doubtful.

For one thing, the horizontally pointing finger might not necessarily be seen by everyone as meaning "the." It might, for example, simply be seen as meaning "one." Or the hand might, indeed, be regarded more as a "hand" than as conveying the idea of specificity.

And what about the cat? Or, we should rather say, what about the cat's *head*? Well, for one thing, people from cultures where small pet cats are unknown but big cats abound might regard the image as, say, the head of a cheetah or even that of a fairly friendly lion. And indeed, someone reading the "universal" sentence might see the cat's head as representing the idea of a "head" more than that of a "cat," and we couldn't really blame them for doing so.

As for the two legs, it's surely doubtful that everyone—or perhaps even a *majority* of people—reading the "universal sentence" would automatically take the two legs to mean the word "walk." The legs might equally well be taken to mean "move," which is a very different concept. We can *move* from Britain to America, but we can't *walk* there, even if we were happy to devote several months to the journey, because we'd drown. Interestingly, the hieroglyph used by the ancient Egyptians to convey the idea of motion was a pair of walking legs not unlike the ones in Sampson's sentence, though the hieroglyph didn't have shoes. In the Valley of the Kings near the Egyptian city of Luxor you can see the walking legs hieroglyph in many places; it was carved by ancient Egyptian pilgrims to indicate they had visited a particular shrine. The very fact that Geoffrey Sampson and the ancient Egyptians attached different, albeit related, meanings to the symbol of the two legs surely shows just how difficult it is to win agreement even over the meaning of an essentially very straightforward symbol like this.

Indeed, would everybody take the "universal" drawing of the legs to mean anything to do with movement at all? Perhaps not. Perhaps some people might wonder where the top part of the body had gone. Again, you might not *yourself* agree with this perception, but I think you could hardly say it was invalid. And if you had never seen a *mat* because you live mainly outdoors and have few home comforts, you might perfectly well interpret Sampson's sentence, drawn in a supposedly universal language, to mean something completely different from what Sampson intended. You might interpret it, for example, as meaning:

> One vicious creature has devoured the top part of my friend but I killed it with an arrow and wrapped its body in cloth.

In practice, there are three reasons why universal writings systems don't work. These are:

1. *The problem of comprehensibility.* As our examination of Geoffrey Sampson's ingenious but ultimately unsatisfactory stab at a universal written sentence suggests, it's highly unlikely that everyone who sees a sequence of drawings or symbols will agree on what the drawings or symbols mean. And even if there were agreement on this, there is no reason for supposing that what the readers take the sequence to mean would necessarily be what the writer of the universal language *intended* the drawing or symbol to mean.

2. *The problem of precision.* The need to distinguish in the example given above between the present and past tense is only one example of the fact that writing only works if it is *precise*. If it isn't, it simply is not going to succeed as a way of communicating the precision of thinking.

And this is the whole point. *This* is the most important reason of all why devising a universal writing system is impossible. The reason is that *we want to set down in our writing precisely the same things that we say when we speak*. And after all, when we speak, we do far more with our language than merely *give names to things*. When we speak, we routinely communicate extremely complex concepts. Indeed, the concepts are so routinely complex that spoken language really is one of the marvels of our species, perhaps even the principal marvel.

For example, a toddler, prone to being naughty and aware of it, might say to his mother, "[If] Mummy give me ice cream, I be good," which would be a pretty straightforward thing for a toddler to say to its mother. But it's not easy to imagine how we could easily set down even this simple concept in a universal writing system.

To return to the example of the cat that strolls over the mat, assuming we did manage to win some sort of universal acceptance for the idea of depicting the concept of "the" by using a pointing finger, we would have to solve other, very basic problems if we were to extend the writing system into anything that would be useful. How do we convey, for example, the notion of "my cat," or even "this cat" as opposed to "that cat"?

We could think of ways to do this, but they would be complex ways, and the more complex our universal writing system becomes, the less likely it would be that everyone could readily understand it. But if you think about it, it's really pretty self-evident that the incredibly complex nuances of spoken language cannot possibly be set down in a would-be universal writing system which merely consists of a series of diagrammatic symbols whose meaning can't even be precisely specified.

The above two reasons show that the idea of a universal writing system is not much more than pie in the sky. But there is a third reason, too, and this really is the final nail in the coffin for the idea of a universal writing system.

3. *The problem of practical convenience.* The simple and unavoidable fact is that it's unrealistic to expect anyone to draw a succession of complex images or symbols each time they want to write anything down. Even with the writing systems we *do* use, writing things down quickly is difficult, which is why specialized writing systems such as shorthand have evolved.

To take just one example, no one is going to have the time to draw an entire cat, or a cat's head, on every single occasion when they want to write the idea of a cat. What would happen, very quickly, is that the cat's head would become simplified and *then* you would need to take care that the cat did not look like a dog, bear, lion, or tiger. You might try to solve this problem by drawing only the cat's whiskers, in the same way that you might try to simplify the task of drawing a pig by only drawing its little curly tail.

But even drawing whiskers (and how do you make sure they look like a cat's whiskers, not a mouse's?) or curly tails requires some artistic skill, and writing systems need to be used by anyone, including people who have no artistic skill at all. And once the drawings start to become simplified so that they can be drawn quickly, you are well on the way to creating images that look nothing at all like the original creature and which may as well be the individual, stylized writing that is only comprehensible to those who have learned it.

Writing systems requiring a high level of artistic ability—the Egyptian hieroglyphic system, for example— were always only practiced by a small minority of the population. The "pure" form of Egyptian hieroglyphs was the sole preserve of priests and scribes who could draw. Two easier-to-draw forms of hieroglyphs—known as hieratic and demotic—eventually developed for use by a somewhat larger (though not vastly larger) proportion of the population.

And in any case, even if we *could* draw easily recognizable pictures of things very rapidly (and we can't), writing needs to do so much more than simply set down pictures of things.

When we speak, we generate complex thoughts automatically for the very simple reason that our speech *reflects* our thinking. Language, like thinking itself, is a habitual process. Imagining that a crude system of visual signs such as the ones Geoffrey Sampson uses will enable you to set down in visible form the incredible subtlety and complexity of language—and I'm not only referring to *marvelous* language such as "Shall I compare thee to a summer's day?"—is like imagining that a photograph of someone you love is anything like as wonderful as the person is.

The point is: Writing systems work by setting down *language* rather than ideas directly. And just as language itself has evolved to allow us to say whatever we want to say, writing systems have evolved to accommodate the needs of *language*, not of the things we want to speak about.

Another type of language and speech that a universal writing system would struggle with is dialect—defined by the *Oxford English Dictionary* (*OED*) as "a form of speech peculiar to a district" or "a variety of language with nonstandard vocabulary, pronunciation, or idioms." Dialect is rarely set down satisfactorily in writing.

For example, the word "new" will typically be pronounced by a Londoner with a *y*-sound just after the *n*, so that the word sounds something like "nyew." A New Yorker, on the other hand, is likely not to include the *y* sound, pronouncing the word something like "noo." But when the word is written the spelling is the same in either case. Similarly, people in the north of England tend to make the *a* sound in the word "bath" a short sound, to rhyme with the vowel sound in "cat." People in the south of England are more likely to make the sound a long one, to rhyme with the vowel sound in "Garth." But again, the same spelling is used in either case.

The most likely reason why writing does not usually bother to distinguish between differences in dialects is that writing is in its very essence designed to be a technology that—like most technologies—can be used as widely as possible, and so it is more convenient if it is a *standard* technology that can be applied to cover the widest range of eventualities.

This is all very well, but much of the best writing in any culture is done by writers who want to emphasize the uniqueness and specialness of a particular regional culture. When they set down the speech of that culture in words, they have a dilemma: Do they try to write down the speech as precisely as possible (to give its true flavor), or do they try to *suggest* what the speech sounds like?

The big problem with writing the speech down as it sounds is that, for most languages, there is no standard and conventional way of writing down regional dialect. Ironically, there often was in the past: Anglo-Saxon, for example, originally had four main regional dialects which all had at various times their own reasonably standardized way of being written down. However, in today's world, most cultures find it far more convenient to have a single national standard for writing a language, even if regional differences in how the language is spoken (sometimes to the extent of incomprehensibility to speakers from other regions) still persist. These "regional differences" include varied pronunciations and vocabulary—and even varied grammatical constructions.

It is true that some of these regional words are included in dictionaries, but one feels that the dictionary's authority to state a particular spelling is not as strong here as it would be in the case of more familiar words.

For example, I was brought up in the British East Midlands, where the word "mardy" was widely used to mean "sullen," "spoiled," or "whining," especially when referring to a child. The *OED* does indeed spell this word as "mardy," but because the word is very much a regional matter, one might perhaps spell it as "mardee" or "mardie" without feeling that the spelling was "wrong."

Some words are beloved of different age ranges, which creates a kind of special dialect constrained by the ages of the people who speak it. For example, children in British playgrounds love to use the word "lurgy" to refer to some unspecified infectious ailment which makes a child who is said to have it an object of pity and revulsion (as in the impassioned and contemptuous childhood cry "He's got the lurgy!"). The *OED* spells the word as "lurgy" and notes that its origin is unknown. However, spelling it as "lurgee" somehow looks more appropriately childlike, sinister, and, well, infectious.

Where writers do ardently wish to set down the dialectical way of speaking because they see it as integral to what they are trying to say, they have little choice but to devise their own way of writing down the dialect. For example, the writer Irvine Welsh, in his powerful novel *Trainspotting*—which tells the story of a group of young people in Edinburgh living in a nightmarish world of drugs, drink, and violence—narrates the entire tale in a dialectical style that is at first difficult to master, but strangely rewarding when you have done so. This is how the book starts:

The sweat wis lashing oafay Sick Boy; he wis trembling. Ah wis jist sitting thair, focusing oan the telly... Ah tried tae keep ma attention oan the Jean-Claude Van Damme video.

As happens in such movies, they started oaf wi an obligatory dramatic opening. Then the next phase ay the picture involved building up the tension through introducing the dastardly villain and sticking the weak plot thegither. Any minute now though, auld Jean-Claude's ready tae git doon tae some serious swedgin.

As well as vigorously drawing the reader into the narrator's strange world, the writing in dialect has the useful purpose here of lending a certain lightness, comedy, and comforting remoteness to this fundamentally sordid scene, in which a sick young man is contemptuously ignored by his friend—the narrator—who only cares about being able to watch an action movie that he himself recognizes as violent rubbish.

The dialect achieves this effect by emphasizing the narrator's viewpoint and winning sympathy for the narrator's self-centered perspective on what is going on. The vitality of the writing is dependent not only on the dialectical spellings (e.g., "wis" for "was," "oafay" for "off," "oan" for "on," and "tae" for "to") but also on the particular vocabulary used. There are many dialect words used in *Trainspotting*: "Swedgin," for example, presumably comes from the word "swedge," first recorded in the mid–eighteenth century and meaning a hammer-shaped tool used by blacksmiths, though it's hardly a common word in modern English.

The dialect writing in *Trainspotting* can be effective, but its unfamiliarity makes it hard work to read, even for people who actually speak in this way, because the dialectical spellings Irvine Welsh uses are substantially his own invention. They inevitably must be, due to the lack of a standardized spelling for Edinburgh dialect. And this shows another problem with dialectical spellings: Because there isn't any accepted standard for spelling them, the spellings have to be improvised by the writer. It's by no means the case that the way one writer spells them will be the way another writer does.

Because of the undoubted difficulty of reading dialect writing, many writers prefer to suggest or imply dialect, aware that if not properly handled, too much unfamiliar dialect speech can alienate the reader. Or the audience—the compelling film adaptation of *Trainspotting* had the narrator's voice-over and the characters' dialogue rendered mainly in fairly standard English.

So writing *can* be used to set down a dialect. But on the whole writing seems best adapted to being a sort of *general* tool to record the standard, widely accepted form of a language rather than a regional variant of it. In much the same way, writing sets down spoken language in a sort of *general* sense rather than reproducing the particular speech patterns and tones of individuals. We *can* convey what those speech patterns and tones are, but only by providing additional information such as the use of italics to provide emphasis and the use of an exclamation mark and a question mark.

Another area where writing in general—and English spelling in particular—is rather inefficient at dealing with spoken language is in how it handles proper names, such as names of people. When the name is established in a language there will be a clear spelling convention that applies. For example, names such as "John," "Helen," and

"Claire" usually obey strict spelling conventions. However, because English is not an especially phonetic language, we usually need to make particular inquiries when finding out the precise spelling of someone's name—"John" can also be spelled as "Jon," and "Claire" as "Clair" or "Clare."

When I visited New York some years ago I had a meeting with a businessman whose surname was spelled "Loofburrow." I asked him about this and he told me his family originally came from Loughborough in England and had adopted the town's name as their surname, but had changed the spelling to something Americans could more readily pronounce, being less likely to be familiar with the word Loughborough. Even where spelling on the whole follows a rigorous standard, there are more gray areas than we might imagine, especially relating to the spelling of names.

And what do we do in English about foreign names that are not even written in alphabetical writing systems? The answer is that a system of romanization is generally used, and these systems can change over time, which is why we nowadays write "Beijing" and "Mao Zedong," rather than the former "Peking" and "Mao Tse-Tung."

In fact, where there is an accepted romanization system, the writing of a foreign nonalphabetic name is fairly straightforward. But a strange-looking name in a foreign language that is written using Roman letters will not have any standardized way of being written. I once lived in a

Finnish city called Jyväskylä, an exciting and vibrant place despite having a name that makes you think of a fish bone caught in your throat. It's not a name that is part of the consciousness of most English speakers, nor is it ever likely to become so, but if it ever did by some strange accident, a standardized spelling would doubtless soon develop based around the sound, something like Youvaskoola. Unfortunately, that looks pretty horrible, too. A better solution in this case might be to translate the meaning of the city's name into English, which would give the much more manageable Corn Village—although it is a city. Still, the name of the German city of Düsseldorf means "village by the Düssel [a river]," and Düsseldorf nowadays has a population of close to 600,000.

We see in all the above that while writing is *necessary* for setting down spoken words, there are clear limits to how *efficient* it is at doing this. But we live with these inefficiencies, partly because of course writing does *far more* than merely set down spoken language. Most writing is not, in fact, done in order to set down spoken language at all. Instead, it is done to set down our *thinking*, which we express in linguistic form even though we don't need to speak it. All the following are examples of writing with which we might typically interact as writers or readers on a day-to-day basis. None of these examples of writing is specifically designed to set down speech:

- shopping list
- medical prescription
- daily newspaper
- telephone directory
- electric bill
- television teletext information
- e-mail
- Internet shopping information
- wall calendar
- the numbers on a clock face
- cooking instructions on food packaging

I have deliberately left one item off this list—mobile telephone text messages. This is because I rather think text messages *are* designed to set down spoken language. We probably do tend to think of the text messages we receive as written forms of our friends' voices. Even if you don't agree with this, it is at least surely undeniable that text messages are more of a "living" kind of writing than the examples listed above.

What about literature? This is a specialized form of writing that is usually composed by just one author and cannot be claimed to set down spoken language, except in the very specialized sense that dialogue is designed to provide a convincing simulation of actual spoken speech. Also, it may be argued that one reliable test of "good" writing is that it is effective when read aloud.

Some forms of literature—short poems, for example, and many forms of writing intended for children—may be designed to be read aloud, but longer works of literature such as adult novels are primarily written, at least nowadays, to be read silently. In the nineteenth century friends and relatives would often read aloud to each other in the evenings. People enjoyed weeping together over particularly sad passages. Many novels—all of Charles Dickens's, for example—were first published in regular installments and only appeared in a single volume once the installments had been issued. Indeed, until the twentieth century, *most* forms of literature were probably designed to be read aloud rather than read silently. Nowadays, being able to read silently is regarded as a sign of intelligence and literacy.

Now is perhaps a good time to summarize some basic observations about the nature of writing. From observing writing in practice and thinking about the function it provides, writing appears to be all of the following:

- Potentially, a way to make a writer "immortal" or at least remembered long after his or her death.
- Varied: There are many ways in which languages can be written down.
- A crucially vital resource, if languages that die out are one day to be revived.
- An effective way of recording how the meanings of words have changed over time.
- A way of recording language on a permanent medium

such as a stone tablet or a semipermanent medium such as paper.

*   A way of recording language on a temporary medium such as slate or a computer screen.
*   A way of recording language in an *extremely* temporary medium such as wet sand on a beach or even trails of smoke in the sky.
*   Primarily a *visible* medium.
*   An artificial technology.
*   As a consequence of this last point, something that must be *learned*.
*   Not a language in itself, but intimately associated with language.
*   A very recent development compared with language itself. I have suggested that modern *Homo sapiens* have existed in their present form for about 100,000 years and that language as sophisticated as the ones spoken today around the world have most likely also existed since that time. But even the very oldest forms of what may be writing do not appear to be more than about 10,000 years old.
*   Something we get emotionally attached to. Once we have mastered a writing system, we are likely to resent changes to the writing system or, at least, likely to feel uncomfortable about them.
*   An arbitrary system, just like language itself.
*   A system allied to a particular language. A universal writing system that can be readily understood by every-

body no matter what their mother tongue or cultural origins appears to be an impossibility.

- A system designed to be comprehensible to speakers of the language in which the writing is composed, and who have taken the trouble to use the system.

- A system that can be written down comparatively easily and quickly. This would seem to preclude very complex drawings being used as writing; they can't be drawn quickly enough.

- A very precise system. Meaning needs to be conveyed accurately and without ambiguity if the writing system is to be efficient.

- A "generic" system for conveying meaning. Writing, as we have seen, does not, on the whole, indicate a particular user's way of speaking.

- A highly demanding system. Writing needs to communicate everything that someone might want to say when they speak. Writing must deal with and handle all the subtle nuances of meaning in human language. It's not enough just to set down names of things.

- Generally, writing tends to be closely allied with the culture of the people who use the writing system in question as well as with the language itself.

- Despite the close connection with language, there are many specialized forms of writing—the notations for mathematics, music, and chess—which are not particularly connected with language. Writing is therefore *more* than merely a way of setting down language.

- Not usually good at dealing with regional variations of language such as dialect. At the very least, there is rarely any standardized way of writing down dialects.
- Not particularly adept at handling foreign names.
- Often done for a very mundane purpose.
- Up until the start of the twentieth century, mainly designed to be read aloud, rather than to be read silently in private.
- Mainly composed by people who are not specialized writers, but just want to use the tool for practical purposes.

Knowing as we now do that a universal language is not, in fact, a realistic possibility, let's move on to conducting an interesting experiment.

Imagine we were trying to invent a workable writing system *from scratch*. How might we do this?

As we saw in the example of the cat walking over the mat (no puns with "scratch" intended), the first and presumably most obvious way to represent visible things is to draw a picture to depict the thing you mean. Realistically, for the reason of practical convenience, you would quickly find that it was much easier for you to draw a house that was more like a *diagram* of a house than a detailed picture of one. Yet whether you are drawing a detailed picture or a diagram, you are still drawing what is basically a picture.

Written representations of physical objects or living creatures are known as *pictograms,* from the Latin *pictus,* meaning "painted," and the Greek -*gram*, meaning "something that is written." The word "pictograph" is also sometimes seen, but "pictogram" is the term most books about writing prefer, so it's the one I'll use here.

Useful as pictograms would be if you tried to write down your spoken language, you'd soon realize that many of the words you wanted to write down couldn't, in fact, easily be translated into pictures. In fact, undoubtedly the actual *majority* of words you want to set down ("undoubtedly," for example) won't be readily capable of being set down as pictures, because as we've seen, language is obviously much more than a mere list of physical objects or living creatures.

Imagine, for example, you wanted to write down the statement "My house is beautiful." Once you've drawn your house, you'd have to think of some way of drawing the ideas of "my" and "beautiful." Setting these more complex concepts down in writing is a great deal more difficult— and what do you do when you want to set down pictures for *really* complex ideas such as, say, "belief" or "fantasy"?

Written representations designed to suggest an idea rather than to evoke a tangible object are known as *ideograms*, from the Greek *ideo*, meaning "idea," and then again the Greek -*gram*. Inventing ideograms that convey their meaning to a reader who has not already learned what the ideogram means is difficult. It may be almost impossible, because by its very nature an idea is an abstract concept.

Both pictograms and ideograms are *logograms*: that is, writing symbols that are designed to convey *meaning*.

Some definitions of "logogram" (including the one in the *OED*, as a matter of fact) define it as something that stands for a "word." But this is not in fact a very helpful definition, because a word—by definition—will always consist of some self-contained meaning, whereas many logograms used in writing systems around the world today in fact represent *elements* of meaning.

If you have two daughters, and I don't know this and ask you about your daughter, you might respond by saying "*-s*": That is, you are communicating to me you have more than one daughter by emphasizing the plural ending of "daughters." That sound you make ("*-s*") can hardly be described as a word, and in fact it isn't one, but that's not to say it doesn't have meaning, because it does.

Today, the world's most popular language whose writing system employs logograms is Chinese. In Chinese, the "characters" (the name given to Chinese logograms) are usually employed to stand for *units of meaning*. But they don't necessarily stand for individual words, and in fact, if you were to set out to learn Chinese—which is hardly a bad idea when the Chinese economy is doing so immensely well—one of the first things you would need to learn is that thinking of characters as standing for words isn't helpful. Instead, you need to think of them as standing for elements of meaning that may not necessarily make any sense on their own: like the "*-s*" at the end of the word "daughters."

This said, very many characters *do* have a self-contained meaning, and may on occasion even look something like the meaning they represent, although most no longer do because their design has become stylized over time. The character for "person," for example, looks like this:

which is basically a representation of the essentially forked appearance of people. (In *King Lear*, Shakespeare has Lear speak in his madness of man as a "poor, bare, forked animal.")

The Chinese writing system frequently combines two or more characters (sometimes into one character, although they may be used side by side) to produce a more complex meaning. For example, the character meaning "love" is a combination of the character for "woman" and the one for "child." Incidentally, the character meaning "quarrel" consists of one character meaning "woman" set next to another one, which presumably says something about what the Chinese think is likely to happen when two women get together.

Because Chinese is a language that is structurally founded on units of meaning, it is very well suited to a writing system based around logograms. In any event, while there have on occasion been various initiatives to try to change the Chinese writing system into one based around an alphabet, these have never come to anything except for romanizations used mainly by non–Chinese people to write down Chinese sounds. Another important reason why attempts to change Chinese into an alphabet-based system have not succeeded is unquestionably that Chinese contains very large numbers of homophones, and indeed in some cases a particular sound in Chinese can have up to about ten different meanings, plus even more if the sound is spoken with a different intonation; Chinese is a language that makes extensive use of tones to define meaning. Alphabet writing systems don't cope well with homophones and often give little or no clue to differences in meaning. A logogram-based writing system, on the other hand, is by its nature well suited to dealing with homophones because it is focusing on their meaning rather than their sound and so clearly distinguishes between the different meanings.

Let's now move on from logograms to the writing systems that focus above all on the *sound* of the language.

This way of writing down a language involves making use of *phonograms*: from the Greek *phono*, meaning "sound" or "voice", and *-gram*. A phonogram (we call them "letters" when we write English) is a written symbol that evokes—again ideally on a consistent basis—a particular sound of a language.

Phonograms are used by *alphabetic* writing systems. The basic idea of any alphabetic system is, at least in theory, to equate written letters with the sound elements of the language in question. In practice alphabetic writing systems differ according to the accuracy and consistency of the relationship between their letters and the sounds of the language.

Interestingly, while it is indeed true that Chinese is primarily a meaning-based writing system, the Chinese writing system also often uses the sound of a character *when it is spoken* in order to give clues to the *sound* of a more complex character that consists of the "sound" character plus a "meaning" character. It's rather as if—for example— we were to put a picture of a shoe next to a picture of a building to write down the idea of "shop" because the *sh*-sound of "shoe" gives a clue to the sound of the word represented by the character combination: This is a special kind of building, one that is a *shop*.

On the face of it, a logographic writing system and a phonographic writing system operate in completely different ways. But as far as the result on the reader of each type of system, there may be more similarities than we would imagine.

A logographic writing system is read by an expert reader making an instantaneous mental link between the shape of one or more logograms and the meaning these have in the writing system. But, in fact, this also appears to be what happens when an experienced reader of an *alphabetic* writing system reads a word that consists of various letters: We recognize the pattern of the visual appearance of the entire word. The fact that, as readers of the

English alphabetic writing system, we do seem to read familiar words in their entirety with one quick visual intake to the brain suggests that English (and other alphabetic writing systems) may operate rather as a kind of logographic writing system after all.

I am not suggesting this applies to every English word you read. Technical words with which you may not be immediately familiar—"logographic," for example—do tend to be read in a phonographic way: That is, we look at the different letters in succession from left to right and decide what the word should sound like. But *familiar* words are a different matter. Does any literate person really read a word like "cat" or "dog"—or any word with which they are very familiar—by carefully looking at the letters from left to right? The answer is no. It's like learning to drive. We start by being conscious of rules we need to follow carefully in sequence—switch on the engine, depress the clutch, move into first gear, release the hand brake, press down on the accelerator a bit, and so on. But when we *know* how to drive we don't go through this process in such a meticulous stage-by-stage way. Instead, we just drive.

I suggested in the previous chapter that in most cases we are able quite easily to read words even if all the letters apart from the first and last letter are jumbled up. This fact seems to add weight to the argument that when we read English, we do so mostly in a *logographic* way.

Let's now take a look at where alphabets come from.

Part Two

—

From A to Z

___

Chapter 3

Alphabets—the Upsides
and Downsides

Letters are the original snap-on tools.

> —David Sacks, *The Alphabet* (2003)

N alphabet is any writing system that uses letters to represent the sounds of a language with
a level of consistency that tends to vary from
one language to another.

Like Chinese, most writing systems that are mainly
logographic do make some use of written symbols to represent sounds of the language. But, it is only reasonable to
call a writing system an alphabet if it only uses letters or
uses letters almost exclusively.

The English writing system is certainly an alphabet,
but whether or not you agree with my belief that we
mostly read in a logographic fashion, our writing system
does give employment to a few logographic symbols. The
ampersand "&," for example, while conveniently spoken
as "and" in English, is strictly speaking not a letter but a
logogram that sets down *meaning* rather than sound. The

same can also be said of figures indicating numbers: "1," "2," "3," and so on.

When the chips are down, or even when they aren't, most of us tend to be fairly tribal in our attitude toward other people and other cultures. This explains why many people are never so happy as when they're proclaiming that the way *they* see things is the *right* way, and that any other way of viewing matters is at best insanity and at worst a crime against nature. This basic observation about human nature goes a long way toward explaining why the world is the way it is and not a whole lot better. And the same observation explains why a good many people who use alphabetic writing systems are only too ready to proclaim that an alphabet is absolutely the best and most perfect way of writing things down.

This tendency is all too evident, even among people who should know better. Bill Bryson, for example, one of the most entertaining and intelligent writers of our generation, does his utmost to persuade us, in the chapter on spelling in his book *Mother Tongue,* of the dire consequences of not having an alphabet. The implication is that any culture whose writing system is *not* an alphabet is in the most desperate position. In particular, he says, if you don't use an alphabet, you are in the diabolical situation of being part of a culture where "there can be no crossword puzzles, no games like Scrabble, no palindromes, no anagrams, no Morse code."

With all respect to you, Bill, these drawbacks really don't seem to me an utterly appalling price to pay for not having an alphabet. Crossword puzzles are fun enough, but I can't imagine anyone will feel their ability to enjoy life *entirely* snuffed out if they can never again indulge in palindromes (words or phrases that spell the same thing forward or backward, such as *able was I ere I saw Elba*, that insightful summary of Napoleon Bonaparte's career) or anagrams (such as *Silly bib, Ron!* for "I, Bill Bryson"). Oh, and talking of palindromes, in case you're interested, the Finnish language has the longest single-word palindrome in the world: *saippuakauppias*, which means "soap-seller."

As for Scrabble . . . is this frustrating game (and a potentially irritating one, too, if you are playing against those determined enthusiasts who spend their spare time learning very obscure and funny-looking words that are never actually used except by such people when they play Scrabble) really worth all the downsides of having an alphabet?

And there *are* downsides of having an alphabetic writing system. In particular:

◆ There is no *visible* connection between the appearance of a word written using an alphabet and the meaning of the word. The visual appearance of the written word therefore provides no direct visual clues as to what the written word means; you can only read the word if you know the alphabet in which it is written.

◆ You can *understand* a word written in an alphabetic writing system only if you know the alphabet in which it is written *and* the language. The fact that many letters used in alphabetic writing systems are used by a wide range of languages means that you may often be able to make a good attempt at *pronouncing* a word written in an unfamiliar language (especially if its writing system is highly phonetic) but will have no idea what it means. For example, the Finnish word *poika* is quite easy to read aloud for anyone who can read English because most of the letters used in Finnish writing are the same as in English and Finnish is a highly phonetic language. But unless you have at least some knowledge of Finnish, you won't know that this word means "boy."

◆ It is usually impossible for the same alphabetic writing system to be capable of being read by people who speak mutually incomprehensible languages or dialects. Yet another great advantage of Chinese characters, which as we've seen are primarily based around writing down units of meaning, is that they can be easily read and understood by people speaking the principal Chinese dialects, all of which are mutually incomprehensible. Similarly, the ampersand logogram means the same whether it is being read by someone whose mother tongue is English, French, German, or indeed any other language whose writing system makes use of the ampersand. But because an alphabet is based around the *sounds* of a particular language, it renders this cross-use of the same written word by mutually incomprehensible languages impossible. Apart from the commonsense observation that we can't understand alphabetic written words of languages we don't know, there are many alphabetic words which mean completely different things in different languages. For example, in German the word *Gift* means "poison," something you would only give to someone you wanted to injure or kill, whereas of course in English it means, by and large, something you give to someone you *like*.

• The fundamental benefit alphabets supposedly offer is that the letters of words written using an alphabetic writing system accurately relate to the sounds of the spoken language and so make the writing system easy to understand, at least if the reader knows the language in which the word is written. But in practice, this benefit will only apply if the way individual words are *pronounced* equates directly with the way they are *written*. In some languages—English is a good example—this is not particularly the case. Furthermore—and this is also an important reason why the English writing system often appears highly unphonetic—it is desirable for the purposes of convenience that a writing system becomes fixed and constant as soon as feasible, but the sounds of a spoken language will always change over time. It follows logically from this that, by and large, the earlier in history an alphabetic writing system became fixed, the less connection there may be now between the system and the way its words are pronounced. As we shall see, the spellings of many English words became fixed about 600 years ago, but the way we *say* the words has changed. This explains, for example, why we write the two words that sound like "nite" as "night" and "knight." Their spellings reflect how they once used to be pronounced. Some languages, and especially

English, are indeed highly unphonetic. When this is the case, the major benefit of using an alphabetic writing system is to some extent negated.

• This "major benefit" may not be very major anyway. Why? Because, for reasons we've already seen, we appear to read familiar words by glancing at the *entire shape* of the word rather than running through in our minds the sequence of letters and the cumulative sounds they represent. This indeed seems to suggest that ultimately we read familiar words in a logographic way.

• Alphabetic writing systems are poor at differentiating between homophones (words that sound the same but have different meanings), because by definition alphabetic writing systems reflect the *sound* of words rather than their *meaning*. So, for example, the word *kurkku* in Finnish means both "throat" and "cucumber," and if you are reading the word you don't have much choice but to use context to work out which meaning is intended. Ironically, it is the very fact that English is a highly unphonetic language that helps to give at least some minor visual differentiation between homophones. Examples are: "gate"/ "gait"; "cocks"/"cox"; and "rough"/"ruff." The sound for which one spelling is "air" has numerous other spellings in English, both as a single word and as part of a compound. These spellings include: "Ayr" (the Scottish seaside town); "e'er"; "ere" (the now largely obsolete word meaning "before"); "heir"; the vowel sound in "square"; and the first syllable in the words "airplane," "Airedale" (as in the dog), and "parent." Some of these similar sounds gave rise to a joke, fashionable about a century ago (this is true of most of my jokes), that ran along the following lines: Q. "What is the difference between a prince, a gorilla, a bald man, and an orphan?" A. "The prince is an heir apparent, the gorilla has a hairy parent, the bald man has no hair apparent, and the orphan has ne'er a parent." Well, those *were* the days before DVDs.

A final point about the less positive side of alphabets is not funny at all. There is evidence that the very fact of a culture using an alphabetic writing system may make the problem of dyslexia more difficult for people who suffer from it. Dyslexia is a neurological disorder that inhibits a person's ability to recognize and process graphic symbols, especially those related to language. Dyslexia is a profound psychological enigma, not least because it usually occurs in people who otherwise have normal—and indeed often exceptional—intellectual skills. Many dyslexic people, for example, have strong artistic and interpersonal capabilities. The causes of dyslexia are still poorly understood, but there is clear evidence that people suffering from the condition are likely to find reading and writing more difficult if their mother tongue is written using an alphabetic system.

The reason for this is that dyslexic people often have problems "seeing" what may seem to nondyslexic people very obvious links between the spellings of words and the way the word is pronounced. Breaking down a word such as "gorilla" into three separate syllables as "go-rill-a" and then saying the syllables aloud is for most people a useful way to learn to spell this and other words. Dyslexic people, however, can often not readily understand—or do not even understand at all—the links between the written syllables and the sound. This is a serious problem for them, because of course this link is exactly what an alphabet is designed to facilitate.

There has been research carried out with dyslexic children that suggests that such children may find learning a logographic writing system such as the Chinese one easier to deal with than an alphabetic system. Even if Chinese characters do not give any obvious visual clue to the meaning of the sound they represent (and the vast majority don't), some dyslexic children seem to find such characters easier to master than alphabetic words because the characters relate to meaning rather than to sound. Further research is continuing into this intriguing matter. Whatever the results of its findings, the research undertaken so far should help shake us out of any complacency that alphabetic writing systems are *inherently* the best way of writing.

The written word "alphabet" is first recorded in English in 1580. It is a borrowing from the Latin word *alphabetum,* which comes from the Greek word *alphabetos.* This Greek word is constructed from the names of the letters "alpha" and "beta": that is, the names of the first two letters of the

Greek alphabet. Today, in modern English, we use those names to refer not only to the two letters of that alphabet but also to the "best" and "second best" of anything.

In general, an alphabet aims to break down the various sounds of a language into their constituent elements. These constituent elements are known as *phonemes*. A phoneme is a meaningful unit of sound in a language that cannot be analyzed into a smaller unit and *which can distinguish both the sound and meaning of one word from another*.

For example, the *p*-sound at the start of the word "pat" is a phoneme in English, just as the *b*-sound at the start of the word "bat" is a phoneme. These sounds are English phonemes because they have an effect on the meaning of a word. Remember, incidentally, that we are talking here about *spoken* words, not written ones. Phonemes are nothing to do with how a language is *written* but rather with how it is *spoken*.

In understanding how alphabets have developed and evolved, it is important to keep two points in mind.

Firstly, remember that all languages are spoken first and only *subsequently* written down, sometimes long after they were first spoken.

Secondly, we need to bear in mind that languages are systems of communication that use spoken sounds which have acquired a meaning to speakers of a particular language. These sounds are simply that: *sounds*. Individual sounds that may incorporate one or more syllables and have a complete, self-contained meaning are called words.

Words are above all something *spoken*, and only secondarily something *written*. It is tempting, but misleading, to think of words as primarily being something written down. It is easily done, but unhelpful, because the whole process of understanding how alphabets work is about understanding how special types of visible marks developed that came to be used by a whole community to represent the spoken sounds that constitute the language.

In the words "pat" and "bat," the *a*-sound and *t*-sound are also phonemes. In the word "ship," there are three phonemes, the *sh*-sound, the *i*-sound, and the *p*-sound. If you lengthen the *i*-sound in "ship" by changing your mouth shape you get another sound, normally represented in writing as *ee*. The result of lengthening the *i*-sound is to produce a completely different word, which is written down as "sheep." Again, we are talking here primarily about sounds of language rather than the spellings.

There is a technical way of writing down phoneme sounds that is entirely unambiguous and which therefore links every phoneme with a unique way of writing it down. This is known as the International Phonetic Alphabet (IPA).

The IPA provides symbols for writing down the phonemes of any known language in the world. The purpose of the IPA is to ensure that one symbol, and one symbol only, is used internationally to represent any given phoneme (i.e., whichever language is being written down), so there is no chance of ambiguity. Because different languages vary in terms of all the different phonemes they use, the range of IPA symbols used for a particular language will differ to some extent from one language to the other. Indeed, there will even be some variation in the IPA used for different dialects of English.

Here are the first three lines of Hamlet's soliloquy, spoken in standard English, and written in the IPA:

Hamlet: /tə biː ɔː nɒ tə biː ðæt ɪz ðə kwɛstʃən
wɛðə tɪz nəʊblər ɪn ðə maɪn tə sʌfə
ðə slɪŋz ən ærəʊz əv aʊtreɪdʒəz fɔːtʃuːn/

Dictionaries routinely use the IPA, or slightly simplified versions of it, when they list a word, in order to show very clearly how the word should be pronounced.

If the IPA were employed to write down English—and there is no practical reason why this could not be done—the problem of the illogicality, irregularity, and even sheer absurdity of English spelling would, at least in principle, disappear overnight. However, it would be replaced by another problem: the need to learn all the new symbols of the IPA as applied to English. *Because* the IPA is designed to avoid ambiguity, it needs to define the sound of each phoneme of English with complete precision. This is why there are forty-four symbols in the IPA for English, eighteen more symbols than there are letters in the English alphabet.

So to use a completely phonetic alphabet for English,

we would need to learn lots of new symbols. Also, if you spoke a dialect of English, the alphabet you learned would not necessarily apply to your own dialect, and this would rather destroy the purpose of using the purely phonetic alphabet in the first place.

We would also lose all the historical and cultural history of our spelling system. To take just one small example, the interesting connections, mentioned above, in the derivation of the very word "alphabet" from Latin and Greek forms would be lost if it were written in a purely phonetic way. These connections are part of our cultural heritage, and of course they do help us to learn the spellings of borrowed words such as "alphabet."

Worst of all, though, purely phonetic writing looks absolutely horrendous, as the physical appearance of Hamlet's speech in the IPA shows all too well. Aren't we really much better off with the usual way of writing it? The IPA looks like a writing system for robots, not for people.

The reason the alphabetic system of writing was such a momentous development in the story of writing is that alphabetic writing systems cleverly—or accidentally— exploit the fact that all human languages only use a relatively small number of individual phonemes.

With the benefit of hindsight—that magical elixir which transforms us all into authorities on everything— it seems "obvious" that, as languages have relatively few phonemes (in fact, languages use between about twenty and forty-five phonemes), any system of writing based around devising written symbols for those phonemes should, at least in theory, be a hugely useful solution to the challenge of how to write words down.

Let's look at some alphabets in action.

In the past, most people—apart from scholars—had little exposure to writing done in languages that were not spoken around them every day. Today, however, we come across a wide range of writing in other languages: on television, in films, on restaurant menus, and of course on all types of packaging. The enormous internationalization of the commercial world means that many manufacturers find it cost-effective to make just one version of packaging for all their importers, with the instructions written in all the languages spoken in the countries where the product is being sold. Manuals for electronic equipment routinely include instructions in more than a dozen languages. The manual for a radio/CD player I once bought is as long as a novella, and includes most western European languages.

A good place to find lots of examples of different writing is the average hotel room, because many hotel rooms around the world have their own copy of a Gideon Bible. More than one billion of these Bibles have been distributed worldwide since the organization Gideons International was founded in 1949. As well as the Old and New Testaments, these Bibles contain, in the early pages, a sentence about Christian religious belief set down in each of the following languages: Afrikaans, Arabic, Chinese,

Danish, Dutch, English, Finnish, French, German, Greek, Hebrew, Hindi, Icelandic, Italian, Japanese, Korean, Malay, Norwegian, Polish, Portuguese, Russian, Sinhalese, Spanish, Swahili, Swedish, Tamil, and Welsh. These twenty-seven languages are understood by about three quarters of the earth's population.

All of these are living languages, but of course much writing has been written in dead languages: Indeed, as we have seen, writing is the only way dead languages can be preserved at all. The sentence *Gallia est omnis divisa in partes tres* ("Gaul is all divided into three parts") with which Julius Caesar started his book *De Bello Gallico* ("Account of the Gallic Wars")—written between 52 and 51 B.C.—is composed in Latin, now a dead language, but it is still very obviously *writing*.

If you lived in the time of the gladiators, and you could read (which didn't necessarily follow), you would have understood the following:

CIVIS ROMANVS SVM

This states one of the proudest boasts anyone could make at the time: "I am a Roman citizen." The literal translation is "Citizen Roman I am." Latin was a language with lots of inflections (modifications to the form of a word that change the word's grammatical function). In Latin, the inflections usually come at the end of a word. Because the inflections of Latin define meaning so precisely, the Romans did not need to be very particular about word order, because the inflections made clear what the word meant. English doesn't have many inflections, so word order matters a lot to us; for instance, "Clair-Marie terrified her suitor" means something very different from "Her suitor terrified Clair-Marie." Only the word order makes the meaning clear.

The enormous political impact of the Roman Empire still resonates around Europe. One of the most obvious resonances is that today almost two billion people in the Americas, Europe, Africa, Oceania, and parts of southeast Asia make use of the Roman alphabet. The modern national alphabets of the western European nations are, strictly speaking, adaptations of the Roman alphabet to Germanic languages (English, German, Dutch, Danish, Norwegian, Swedish, Icelandic, etc.), Romance (French, Italian, Spanish, Portuguese, etc.), Slavic (Polish, Czech, Slovak, etc.), Baltic (Lithuanian and Latvian), and even languages of the Finno-Ugrian language family that are not actually Indo-European at all—languages such as Hungarian, Finnish, and Estonian. Even the international language Esperanto (perhaps for obvious reasons, a more popular interest outside the English-speaking world than within it) is written in the Roman alphabet. In fact, the Roman alphabet is used today for writing every modern European language except Russian and a few related Slavic languages that use the Russian (Cyrillic) alphabet, and Greek, which of course uses the Greek alphabet. Modern English does not bear much resemblance to Latin, but many English words we use today are lifted from Latin, sometimes without the spelling being changed at all, or very little. Examples are *aqua, audio, duo, luna,* and *terra.*

It is also fair to point out that in some cases there have been internal political movements, in countries that did not start out using the Roman alphabet, to move toward using it. These movements seem to arise because of a feeling (which may be entirely irrational) that adapting the Roman alphabet will help to "modernize" a country and to bring it more in line with the forward progress of western civilization. Perhaps the most spectacular example of this belief is Turkey, which in 1928, under the leadership of Ataturk, adopted a slightly modified version of the Roman alphabet to replace the use of the Arabic one. Ataturk firmly believed in modernizing Turkey and bringing the country in line with western European ways, even to the extent of encouraging Turks to discard the fez and traditional Turkish clothing and to wear Western suits instead. The population did not immediately welcome the new alphabet, but Ataturk was insistent. By 1930 the process of replacement and acceptance had been completed, and today Turkish is written in its own version of the Roman alphabet. The Turkish alphabet uses two vowel letters and three consonant letters that employ diacritical marks to distinguish these sounds. There is also a distinction in reverse: a letter *i* without a dot, to indicate a particular sound used in Turkish but not otherwise accommodated by the Roman alphabet at all.

Incidentally, if you speak modern Italian, French, Spanish, Portuguese, or Romanian, you are, strictly speaking, using a modern form of "Vulgar" Latin—the collo-quial form of Latin spoken by Roman soldiers and the working class of Rome. The Classical Latin word for "head," for example, was *caput* (from which modern English words such as "capital" derive), but the slang word was *testa*, meaning "pitcher," from which the French word *tête* ("head") originates. French is in many respects surprisingly similar to Vulgar Latin; we can almost regard modern French as a form of Vulgar Latin spoken in the twenty-first century, and this is in no way to malign the wonderful expressiveness of the French language and its rich literary heritage.

To return to English, let's now explore where exactly the English alphabet came from, and how it developed into what it is today.

Chapter 4

Where Our Alphabet
Came From

[At Harrow] I got into my bones the essential structure of the ordinary British sentence—which is a noble thing. And when in after years my schoolfellows who had won prizes and distinction for writing such beautiful Latin poetry and pithy Greek epigrams had to come down again to common English, to earn their living or make their way, I did not feel myself at any disadvantage. Naturally I am biased in favour of boys learning English. I would make them all learn English: and then I would let the clever ones learn Latin as an honour, and Greek as a treat.

—Winston Spencer Churchill,
My Early Life (1930)

THE modern English alphabet uses twenty-six alphabetical letters to represent the forty-four phonemes of spoken English. The alphabet represents those phonemes effectively enough: After all, the English writing system obviously *works*; English speakers don't go around saying they absolutely refuse to write in English until a more logical writing system is developed. Still, the modern English alphabet doesn't represent the phonemes of modern English with much logic, consistency, or rationality. If the English writing system works, it's *in spite* of the particular nature of the English writing system rather than *because* of it.

Generally, from its earliest days, the English alphabet can be said to have begun with good intentions, but to have become more and more illogical in its application as it needed to deal with a variety of major challenges. These included:

• The fact that, in the very first place, the language whose alphabet English borrowed did not contain certain sounds that are used in English.

• The English spelling system needed to set down an increasingly large number of borrowings from foreign languages. As we have seen, the spelling system has tended to do this by retaining the original or near-original spelling of the borrowings in most cases.

• English spelling became more or less fixed a long time ago, when the pronunciation of English words was still changing. Further changes in the pronunciation of spoken English created an even greater divergence between the spelling of the written word and the way it was pronounced.

The result of these three factors—the implications of which we have already touched upon—and other factors we've still to examine is that today, modern English spelling features what often seems an almost absurd lack of common sense and consistency. One can certainly see a kind of *basic* logic in the way the English alphabet represents sounds, but beyond that, mayhem breaks loose and pretty well everything is, so to speak, up for grabs.

The truth of the matter is that the modern English alphabet uses all the main vowel letters—*a, e, i, o,* and *u*—to stand for just about every possible different vowel phoneme. It also uses combinations of vowels to represent a wide range of diphthongs (that is, vowel combinations such as the *ay*-sound in the word "day") in the most *extraordinarily* inconsistent manner. Furthermore, even consonants aren't immune from the illogicality and inconsistency of how the modern English alphabet works. To take just one example, the letters *gh* are often used to write a final *f*-sound in words that derive from old Germanic forms which ended in a harsh, throatal sound that was a little like a short, hard cough. English used the letters *gh* to set down a sound that was written both in Old English (Anglo-Saxon) and in Old High German (the ancestor of modern German) more straightforwardly with an *h*. However, the use of a final *h* in such words did not sit easily with the English spelling system as it evolved, and so *gh* was preferred. Meanwhile, the actual *sound* at the end of a word such as "rough," which was written both in Old English and Old High German as *ruh,* continued to change until, today, it sounds like the *f*-sound in "fuss."

This one example of how an apparently inconsistent

and illogical spelling in modern English spelling can be explained by looking at it in a historical context provides a key for understanding just *why* modern English spelling is, on the face of it, so crazy. We need to go back in time and look at where the English language and alphabet came from in the first place.

Between about A.D. 450 and 500, Britain was invaded by Germanic tribes called Angles, Saxons, and Jutes. The Britain they were invading was the last vestiges of Roman Britain, in a state of exhaustion and decrepitude. The Roman legions had left Britain in A.D. 410, though no doubt many Romans who had settled in Britain remained there afterward, feeling they were fairly safe. And they were, at least for the time being.

The people with whom the remaining Romans shared Britain at the time of the Anglo-Saxon invasion were Celts, who had first migrated to Britain in significant numbers in the eighth century B.C. The Celts had contin-ued their migration and had gradually assimilated the indigenous Neolithic inhabitants of Britain. Nothing is known about the language or languages spoken by those indigenous inhabitants, though it is possible that some modern British place-names may echo the names used by these pre-Celtic peoples of Britain. Some scholars believe that the Basque language—still spoken in the Basque re-gion of Spain and unrelated to any other known language—may be a survivor of Neolithic days, but this doesn't mean it necessarily has any relationship to the language spoken in Britain before the Celts arrived.

Not a great deal, in fact, is even known about the language spoken by the Celts at the time of the Germanic invasion, except that this language (which probably had several regional dialects) evidently gave birth to the modern Celtic languages Welsh, Irish, and Scots Gaelic. Often referred to as British, the language was a member of the Celtic branch of the Indo-European language family.

The Celts were a learned, cultured people who had lived in relative harmony with the Romans after being conquered by them in A.D. 43, after several small invasions. Some prosperous Celts were bilingual in Latin and British and enjoyed a high standard of living, including access to running water in their homes and even a form of central heating. The Celts were Christian, and probably viewed the invading Germanic tribes as uncivilized, smelly pagans.

But unfortunately for the Celts and those Romans who remained, the Germanic invaders—smelly and pagan as they might have been—were good at fighting, and were also surprisingly able administrators. They quickly took over most of Britain south of the Firth of Forth in Scotland. They left only a few defended areas in the mountainous west of Britain—the regions now known as Wales and Cornwall—and Scotland in the far north, where they had enough sense not to venture.

Celts and Romans who remained in the regions conquered by the Anglo-Saxons were generally killed or enslaved; not surprisingly, most Celts and Romans took to their heels and their hills, moving west or northward. The Celtic language had been the dominant language in Britain before the Germanic invasion. Its tradition now shifted to the remote corners of the British Isles, where it remains to this day.

Today, Celtic traditions are well preserved in the Welsh language, which has held up against English and is still spoken by almost 600,000 people in Wales. Welsh thrives as a language, is taught extensively in schools, and is a language of administration in Wales on equal terms with English. Nowadays, though, with very few exceptions, the only people who are able to speak *only* Welsh are preschool children of Welsh-speaking families, as all children in Wales learn English at school.

In Scotland, Scots Gaelic is today spoken as an everyday language by about 70,000 people, though in general Scots Gaelic does not seem as well entrenched as Welsh.

As for those Celtic Britons who fled to the district now known as Cornwall, they also preserved their language for many centuries, but Cornish has died out as an everyday language. The last native speaker of Cornish, Dolly Pentreath, is buried in a churchyard near the tiny and very beautiful seaside village of Mousehole, close to Penzance. Dolly died in December 1777. Cornish was her mother tongue and the language she preferred to speak, although reportedly she could also speak good English. Today, Cornish is taught in many schools in Cornwall, and some Cornish words are still used locally as dialect words.

Emmet, for example, meaning "ant," is used rather disparagingly by some Cornish people to refer to the hordes of modern-day Anglo-Saxon tourists who swarm into Cornwall in the summer, eating huge quantities of pasties and complaining about the poor mobile telephone service in Cornwall's remote coves.

The language the Anglo-Saxons brought with them was a Germanic tongue closely related to (and probably mutually comprehensible with) Old High German. This German tongue was spoken by the Angles, Saxons, and Jutes and is conveniently known as Anglo-Saxon.

From the moment the Germanic tribes set foot in Britain, their language became Old English. I prefer the term "Anglo-Saxon" because this makes entirely clear that it was the language of the invaders, spoken in Britain. The Anglo-Saxon spoken in Britain remained much the same as the version spoken back home for a century or so, then started to diverge, mainly because in those days, when a migrating people moved several hundred miles (including of course a boat ride if you were going to Britain), not many of them wound up going home for visits. Had they done so, the Germanic language spoken in Britain might have remained more similar to the one spoken on the Continent, just as the close cultural contacts between Britain and the United States since the Declaration of Independence have conspired to keep British English and American English so much alike that, while there are certainly many differences between them, they are unquestionably the same language.

At about the same time when the Anglo-Saxons invaded Britain, another country, just across the Channel, was also invaded by unwelcome visitors. This was Roman Gaul—the country mainly covered today by modern France—and it was invaded by another Germanic tribe, the Franks, who give modern France its name. The curious thing, though, was that unlike the Anglo-Saxons, the Franks soon discarded their own Germanic language— also closely related to Anglo-Saxon—after their invasion of Gaul. Instead of making Frankish the dominant language in Gaul after their invasion, they quickly became assimilated culturally and adopted the Vulgar Latin that was spoken by the inhabitants of Gaul. This, as we have seen, was the ancestor of French.

The end of Roman power in Britain didn't involve a sudden Roman retreat from Britain; rather what happened was that links between the Romans in Britain and the crumbling empire back home became weaker and weaker until, in 410, the remaining Romans told the local governments in English cities to provide for their own defense. Many Romans went home at around this time, to try their fortunes in a similarly chaotic, but at least warmer, land. But by no means did all Romans return; many had married Celts and had made Britain their home.

And so, when the Anglo-Saxons invaded, they encountered not only Celts but also Romans. They found Latin being spoken quite extensively by Romans and by educated Celts. But there was not the same process of linguistic assimilation of the Germanic invaders in Britain as there was in France. One reason was that Latin was by this time nowhere near as significant a language in Britain as it still was in Gaul. This is why modern English derives not from Latin but from Anglo-Saxon and is consequently a Germanic language.

Another factor in the rapid Germanization of Britain was that Celts and Romans driven from the British heartland had somewhere to run to and used the opportunity to flee to the extreme regions of Britain, leaving much of the rest of Britain in the unopposed hands of the invaders. The close linguistic relationship in Britain between Celtic languages at this time and Latin reflects the closeness of the social contacts between these two peoples. Welsh, for example, features many borrowings from Latin.

Across the Channel in Gaul, however, the lack of places to hide meant that the large local Roman population was obliged to stick around and perform the bidding of the invaders, until gradually the Franks were assimilated into the Roman culture.

Once the Anglo-Saxons had dealt with those Celts and Romans who had unwisely elected to fight, they settled down and began to develop societies. While their culture and intellectual life were a good deal more robust and worthwhile than the Celts and Romans imagined, the fact remained that building complex towns and cities was not the Anglo-Saxons' strong point. They tended to live in fairly basic wooden and thatched dwellings which had not changed very much since Neolithic times.

The Anglo-Saxons usually built their towns by rivers and in other favorable locations that had also proved appealing to the departed Romans. Because of this, among the expanding Anglo-Saxon settlements, abandoned Roman buildings stood as mute testament to the fallen glories of the Roman Empire. The Anglo-Saxons retained a respect for these buildings; Anglo-Saxon literature is full of references to what the Anglo-Saxons describe as the "great works" of the past. In my hometown, Canterbury, for example—whose Anglo-Saxon name was originally *Cant ware burg,* or "borough of the men of Kent"—the Roman amphitheater is believed to have been visible, though in a ruined condition, throughout the entire period of Anglo-Saxon rule—that is, until the end of the eleventh century. But the damp and cold English climate eventually ravaged these and other Roman ruins, which is why in Britain today there are no Roman ruins that even remotely compare with the quality of those preserved in the warm, dry European and north African countries beside the Mediterranean.

Now let's look at Anglo-Saxon spelling.

The first thing to say is that the Anglo-Saxons were proud of their language and culture and even brought their own alphabet to Britain. This was not, however, the alphabet with which we are familiar today, but an alphabet known as *runes.*

Runes are often seen today in computer games or in movies that seek to bring alive the mysterious, magical, and sinister past of the Germanic peoples. J. R. R. Tolkien, author of *The Lord of the Rings* (who was a professor of Anglo-Saxon at Oxford University), used runes in his illustrations for the book. One Anglo-Saxon use of runes was to write magical spells (always an important application of writing in the distant past). Runes were a straightforward writing system that used the alphabetic principle. They were adapted to the sounds of Germanic speech and were shaped in an angular fashion for easy carving into wood, which was effectively the dominant writing material of forested Europe in the pre-paper age.

The word "rune" in modern English originally comes from the Old Norse word *runar* (plural *runir*), which meant secret or hidden lore, runes themselves, or magical signs. The word is an instant link back to the past when writing was a magical thing and acknowledged as such very readily within a community. In modern Scandinavian languages the word *rune* means "rune" in the English sense, but there is also a dialect word in Norwegian, *runa,* which means "a secret formula" and provides a verb "to cast a spell." In German today the related word *raunen* means "to whisper"—further proof of the secretive nature of the meanings connected with the runes. There was an English word *roun* (pronounced like "rune"), which meant "a whisper," but it has been mainly obsolete since the Middle Ages, although it is sometimes used in Scots English. There is a Finnish word *runo,* meaning "poem," which also apparently derives from the Old Norse *runar.* The notion of a word like "rune" meaning "secret" crosses language families. For example, the Old Irish word *rún* means "a secret," and Old Irish, like modern Irish, is a member of the Celtic language family.

A variety of runic alphabets survive. One of the best known is the "futhark," which is a word composed from the first six letters of the runic alphabet, namely *f, u, th, a, r,* and *k.* The word "futhark" has been composed just like the word "alphabet" itself, which—as we have seen—is named after the first two letters of the Greek one.

Here are the letters of the futhark runic alphabet after it was adapted by the Anglo-Saxons:

ᚠ ᚢ ᚦ ᚨ ᚱ ᚲ ᚷ ᚹ
ᚾ ᚺ ᛁ ᛄ ᛇ ᛈ ᛉ ᛋ
ᛏ ᛒ ᛖ ᛗ ᛚ ᛝ ᛟ ᛞ

It isn't known for certain where runic script came from originally. Some scholars think it may have been created by a Germanic people living in the Alps around 300 B.C. and that the runes were ultimately derived from the alphabet of a language known as Etruscan, which was spoken by an Italic people at around the time of ancient Rome. The Etruscans had their own alphabetic system, but their language has never been deciphered. An Etruscan dice has survived, marked with the numbers in Etruscan writing, but scholars do not even agree which numbers are which.

Runes became an important alphabet form for the Germanic languages and appear to have been used for business and private correspondence, as well as for writing magical spells: in other words, for pretty well all the main uses of writing by ancient peoples. Unfortunately, there are few examples of runes remaining nowadays; wood, unlike clay or stone, does not keep very well. A total of about 5,000 inscriptions in Germanic runes have survived, but they all tend to be very short. They include carvings on memorial stones and rather tedious declarations of ownership scratched onto metal objects. There are only seventy runic inscriptions remaining from Anglo-Saxon Britain. Probably the most famous one can be seen on what is known as the Ruthwell Cross, in the church at Ruthwell, a village in Dumfriesshire, Scotland. The cross is thought to date to the late seventh century. Though the cross is damaged, it preserves sixteen lines, written in runic, of a famous Anglo-Saxon poem, "The Dream of the Rood," which survives today in Anglo-Saxon. (A "rood" was an Anglo-Saxon word meaning "cross.") "The Dream of the Rood" is believed to be the first poem ever written in English.

By about A.D. 600, the runic alphabet used by the Anglo-Saxons was well on its way to being overshadowed by the Anglo-Saxons' decision to start writing their language in the *Roman* alphabet.

The alphabet used by the Romans to write down their language, Latin, contained the following twenty-three letters:

ABCDEFGHIKLMNOPQRSTVXYZ

In addition, the letters AE were often written as one, as in a name such as "Cæsar."

The Anglo-Saxons borrowed this alphabet to write down their own language. The Anglo-Saxon alphabet was as follows. It is usual to set down the Anglo-Saxon alphabet in lowercase, because at the time when Anglo-Saxon was written down, the letters were mainly (but not always) written in lowercase form. So here is the Anglo-Saxon alphabet:

abcdefghilmnoprstuwxyþðæ

As you see, the Anglo-Saxons did not make use of *j, q,* or *v,* and in practice they used *k* and *z* very rarely (even the Romans had only used these letters to write down Greek names). In fact, *k* and *z* are not usually listed as letters of the Anglo-Saxon alphabet.

The Anglo-Saxons also added two letters of their own, both of which derived from their runes. The letters were necessary additions to the Roman alphabet because the voiced and unvoiced *th*-sounds (see below for examples of these) that were so important in Anglo-Saxon—just as they are so important in modern English—were not used at all in Latin.

One letter was known as thorn by the Anglo-Saxons and is still referred to by this name today. It looked like this in uppercase, Þ, and like this in lowercase, þ.

The other letter looked like this in uppercase, Ð, and like this in lowercase, ð. This letter is nowadays known as eth, but this name was not in fact coined until the nineteenth century. During the Anglo-Saxon period this letter was known as *ðæt*.

This word incorporates the third letter—æ, or "ash"—the joined-together *a* and *e,* which were borrowed by the Anglo-Saxons from Latin. It is in fact still sometimes seen today in Latin borrowings, especially proper names, although modern usage tends to favor the more simple *ae.* (There was originally a third runic Anglo-Saxon letter, known as *wyn,* used to write the *w*-sound not catered for by the Roman alphabet, but it looked very much like thorn and so was soon abandoned and replaced by *w.*)

The curious thing about the letters thorn and eth is that, with two letters available to represent two distinct sounds, common sense would tell us to expect that the Anglo-Saxons would have used the letters in a highly polarized way, with one letter representing one *th*-sound and another letter representing the other. But this is not what happened.

Instead, strangely enough, Anglo-Saxon scribes tended to use thorn and eth interchangeably to denote *both th*-sounds.

For example, the great Anglo-Saxon poem *Beowulf,* which was composed by an unknown poet in the first half of the eighth century A.D., uses the following four spellings to spell the Anglo-Saxon word for "since." This Anglo-Saxon word sounded something like "sithan," with the *voiced th*-sound in the middle:

syþþan

syþðan

syðþan

syððan

That is, every permutation is used somewhere in *Beowulf.* In general, up to about the time of Alfred the Great, who reigned in the Saxon kingdom of Wessex from A.D. 871 to 899, eth was the more common choice to represent both types of *th*-sound, although thorn was still often used. In Alfred's own writing (a sample of which is given later in this chapter), he uses only eth and does not use thorn at all. After the time of Alfred, thorn started being the more common choice, but mainly for the initial position in the word; otherwise eth was still generally preferred.

If this sounds confusing, it is. However, in Old Norse— the language spoken by the Vikings and the language from which the modern north Germanic languages Icelandic,

Faroese (spoken in the Faroe Islands), Norwegian, and Swedish descend—the use of thorn and eth was regularized.

In Old Norse, eth was used only for the *voiced* version of the *th*-sound (as in "this"), while thorn was used only for the *unvoiced* version (as in "thin" or of course in the word "thorn" itself). The fact that the letter eth contains the *unvoiced th*-sound but that the letter itself was used in Old Norse to write the *voiced th*-sound hardly helps matters. Maybe alphabets are not always such a brilliant idea after all.

The clear polarization of Old Norse also applies in modern Icelandic, which still uses the letters eth and thorn. If you go to Iceland, you will see these letters being employed in writing in just as much of an everyday, matter-of-fact manner in which we use *th* in English today. Just to recap exactly *how* these two letters are used, let's join the character Callum Pope—the hero of Zane Radcliffe's entertaining romantic thriller *The Killer's Guide to Iceland*—in his first, brief, Icelandic language lesson. In this scene, Callum's friend Sigriður—the mother of his beautiful Icelandic girlfriend Birna—is doing her best to help him understand his girlfriend's mother tongue, but not getting very far:

"Let us start with the basics," said Sigriður. "The Icelandic alphabet has thirty-two letters. It is the only alphabet that still uses runic symbols. For example there is *eth*, which is written as a *d* in Roman script but has a stroke placed through the stem." Sigriður pulled Callum's unmarked A5 notepad over to her side of the kitchen table. She drew the symbol ð onto the blank page in soft, dark pencil. "This is pronounced as a hard *th* sound, as in *that*. It is not to be confused with the symbol *thorn* which is written like an extended *þ* and is also pronounced with a *th* sound, only it is a softer, more elongated *th*, as in the word *thing*." Sigriður drew the symbol *þ* onto the pad. "Callum, you look at me like I am a madwoman."

"I'm sorry, it's just I now realize that there are three things that are impossible to do in Iceland."

"And what are those things?"

"It's impossible to climb a tree, be a vegetarian, or learn Icelandic."

In English, the visually complex letter eth did not survive the dawn of printing in 1476. The first printers, for convenience, generally preferred to print *th* both for the voiced and unvoiced dental fricative. However, while the simplicity of typesetting *th* was certainly favored by most printers, some were prepared to continue longer with the letter thorn. But printers frequently wanted to avoid the complexity of creating a letter þ or þ, so the job of representing thorn was often given to the capital Y. This was because Y most closely appeared to resemble thorn, although sometimes, as a kind of English compromise, the

---

th-sound was represented by *Dh* or *dh*. Printers used it mainly to represent the *voiced* sound (the *th*-sound in "this"), so they were using thorn in exactly the opposite way to how it was employed in Old Norse and how it is used today in modern Icelandic.

The "Y thorn" is occasionally found in print as late as the eighteenth century, when it was finally entirely superseded by *th*. But it was sometimes seen in handwriting until the nineteenth century.

You can see examples of the Y thorn today on gravestones dating until around the first decade of the nineteenth century. The Y thorn survived on gravestones a little later than it did in print. This was probably because stonemasons carving gravestones found the Y thorn useful as it took up less space horizontally than *th*. They often made the word "the" by carving a Y thorn in the bottom half of the space available for the word and then by adding an *e* in the top half of the space.

By the early nineteenth century, the Y thorn had by and large vanished even from gravestones. But it still survives today in one context: It is used to create an impression of mock antiquity in the names of pubs, restaurants, and cafés which, no matter how new they might be, wish to appear venerable, traditional, and archaic. When you see a sign saying, for example, "Ye Olde Tea Shoppe" (here the extra *e*'s and the doubled *p* consonant contribute to the impression of spurious antiquity), the "Ye" does not mean "ye" (the old plural form of "you," still used in some hymns and carols) but is in fact our old friend the Y thorn. And so here "Ye" means, simply, "The" and should be pronounced like that.

Why exactly did the Anglo-Saxon alphabet derive from the Roman one? Why did the Anglo-Saxons decide to write down their language in the spelling system used by Romans, whom they had so efficiently and comprehensively supplanted in Britain?

The answer is: *religion*.

Once the Anglo-Saxons had completed their invasion, the Romans were no longer a power in Britain. But the Romans themselves had converted to Christianity in the second decade of the third century A.D., following the conversion of their emperor Constantine. The precise date of his conversion is not known, but it is clear that by A.D. 313 he was a committed Christian. Like many converts to anything, the Roman Christians were zealous proselytizers, and for two centuries now, Roman missionaries—most of them highly educated and passionately religious men—had roamed the outer regions of Europe, seeking converts.

The Anglo-Saxons were converted to Christianity by the fabled Roman missionary (and later first archbishop of Canterbury) Saint Augustine, who had traveled to Britain in A.D. 597 with forty missionaries. Saint Augustine had his first success in Kent, when he converted the Kentish King Ethelbert I. Gradually the work of conversion spread throughout Anglo-Saxon Britain. The Anglo-Saxons, true to their basic nature, seem to have regarded Christianity in fairly opportunistic terms; they apparently took to it mainly because it offered the prospect of an afterlife rather than because it would necessarily make them better people. But once they had adopted Christianity, they discarded their former pagan practices and became ardent Christians.

Following their conversion, the Anglo-Saxons almost immediately started using the Roman alphabet—that is, the alphabet of the language in which their new Holy Scripture was written—as their own alphabet, given the modifications discussed earlier. Some Anglo-Saxon scholars, in particular the Venerable Bede, who lived from A.D. 672 or 673 to A.D. 735, became leading Christian scholars, though they tended to write their scholarly works in Latin rather than Anglo-Saxon.

The oldest surviving writing in Anglo-Saxon written in the Roman alphabet comes from around the year A.D. 600. It consists of a few biblical passages, translated from Latin. This oldest writing was followed by an abundance of writing in Anglo-Saxon, and in the Roman alphabet. The writing that has survived to the present day is found almost entirely in manuscripts that are copies of lost manuscripts rather than originals.

One of the most interesting pieces of Anglo-Saxon writing was written by King Alfred the Great himself. Alfred was a remarkable leader. Born in A.D. 849, he lived for just fifty years, yet he probably had more impact on

Anglo-Saxon Britain than any other person—except perhaps William the Conqueror two centuries later.

Alfred's legacy in popular history as the Anglo-Saxon king who burned the cakes does the man great injustice. This strange legend is first found in a tenth-century book *Life of St. Neot,* written in Latin in Britain by an unknown author. I can't help thinking that the legend of the cake burning is simply too outlandish not to be true: I mean, if you were going to *invent* something about Alfred, you'd invent something else. Even if Alfred may have been prone to episodes of absentmindedness in which he failed to remember to take mundane things such as cakes out of the oven, he was a brilliant administrator and a superb military leader. He also developed a code of laws that played a key role in Anglo-Saxon life after around the middle of the ninth century. Yet what I've always found fascinating about Alfred is that even in the midst of his incredibly busy life as a king, warrior, head of government, and religious leader, he still found time to devote himself to nurturing the quality of learning and education in his kingdom. Indeed, judging from what he himself says, he is especially passionate about this.

Alfred, being a deeply religious man, readily shared the contemporary view that the raids he and his subjects had suffered from the Vikings in recent years were a divine punishment from God for the sins of the Anglo-Saxon people. Moreover, Alfred, like many learned Anglo-Saxons, regarded as one of the greatest sins of his people the general decline of learning that he believed had set in over the previous few centuries. And so, in the lulls he enjoyed from having to fight the Vikings, he encouraged the development of scholarship and learning at his court and invited notable scholars from the regions of Mercia, Wales, and the European continent.

Alfred practiced what he preached. He took vigorous steps to improve his own knowledge of Latin—which of course was by then no longer an everyday language in England—and he began to translate Latin books into English in A.D. 887. He also gave instructions that all young freemen in Anglo-Saxon Britain of adequate means must learn to read what he called "English" (he meant Anglo-Saxon, of course). As a further example of practicing what he preached, Alfred took energetic steps to make good reading material *in the everyday language of the Anglo-Saxons* available to the new generation of scholars he wanted to nurture.

Alfred translated into the Anglo-Saxon vernacular several great works of his day from the Latin in which they had been composed. These works included the *Ecclesiastical History of the English People*, written by the Anglo-Saxon historian Bede, and the *Pastoral Care* of Saint Gregory I, the great sixth-century pope, whose book provided a manual for priests in the instruction of their flock.

We gain a wonderful insight into Alfred's own motivations for making these various translations in a remarkable piece of writing, dating from about A.D. 890, that is full of revelations about Alfred's attitude toward scholarship and the importance of the written word. It's one of those pieces of writing that make you realize with completely fresh awareness that history isn't merely some dry, formal chronicle of the past, but that it consists of the accounts of the lives of real, breathing living people who simply happen no longer to be alive.

The piece of writing is Alfred's preface to his translation of *Pastoral Care*. In those pre-printing days, books had to be individually written by hand and were consequently extremely expensive. Alfred's preface was in effect a kind of circular letter sent out with each handwritten copy of the translation. Each copy was intended for a different cathedral or leading church in Alfred's kingdom. The name of the particular bishop who would be sent the translation appeared in the first line of the preface. The name of the bishop in the manuscript of the surviving preface is Waerferth, who was bishop of Worcester. Unfortunately, it's not known how many translations of *Pastoral Care* Alfred ordered altogether.

Whether the preface was really composed by Alfred himself is a moot point. The noted Anglo-Saxon scholar Sir Christopher Ball thinks it unlikely Alfred would have written the preface personally, and that it is far more plausible he would have delegated the job to one of his scholarly assistants. Furthermore, Sir Christopher considers the style of the Anglo-Saxon in the preface stilted, and thinks it very likely the preface was initially drafted in Latin and then rendered on a fairly word-by-word basis into Anglo-Saxon. There is in fact a reference in the preface to the craft of translation, though this does not provide any evidence either way that the preface *itself* was a translation.

Here is the text of the preface in my own fairly free modern English translation. To provide an idea of what Anglo-Saxon writing actually looked like, the translated passage in bold appears in its original Anglo-Saxon form immediately after my modern translation. I have also deliberately left my translation of the bolded passage in the style of the original Anglo-Saxon, which is indeed fairly stilted.

King Alfred sends greetings to Bishop Waerferth with affectionate and friendly words. I would declare to you, Bishop, that it's very often come to my mind what wise men there were formerly throughout the English people, both in sacred and in secular orders; and how there were happy times then throughout England.

I would also remark that the kings who ruled over the people in those days were obedient to God and his messengers, and that the kings maintained their peace and their morality and authority at home, and also enlarged their territory abroad; and prospered both in warfare and in wisdom. And I would tell you how zealous the sacred orders were about teaching and about learning and about all the services they had to perform for God; and I'd remind you how men from abroad came here to this land in search of knowledge and instruction, and how *we*, now, should have to get such knowledge and instruction from abroad, if we were to have them.

So complete was the decay of Latin among the English people that there were very few this side of the [River] Humber who could understand Latin church services, or even translate a letter from Latin into English. I also doubt there were many beyond the Humber who could do this.

In fact, there were so few people who could understand Latin properly that I can't even bring to mind *a single one* south of the Thames when I succeeded to the kingdom. Thanks be to Almighty God we now have an ample supply of teachers! And therefore I command you to do what I believe you would wish to do yourself, that is: Disengage yourself as often as you can from the affairs of this world, so that you can apply the wisdom which God has given you wherever you are able to apply it.

Think what punishments came upon us in this world when we neither loved ourselves nor extended love to other men—we loved to think of ourselves as Christians, and yet very few of us really loved the virtues of our faith.

Well, Bishop, when I brought all this to mind, then I also thought of how, before the ravages of the Viking invasion, I'd seen how the churches throughout all England stood filled with treasures and books. I also recalled how there was a great multitude of God's servants [i.e., priests] in the churches, yet they could draw hardly any benefit from these books. Why? *Because they couldn't understand anything of them*, since they were not written in English.

It was as if these people had said, "Our forefathers who formerly held these places loved knowledge, and through it they acquired scholarly wealth and they left it to us. One can see their footprints here still, but we cannot follow after them and therefore we have lost both the wealth and the knowledge because we didn't take the trouble to master Latin."

When I brought all this to mind, I was—frankly—amazed at those wise men who formerly existed throughout the English people and had fully studied all those books but yet had not wished to translate any part of them into English: their own language! But then I immediately answered my own question and said: "Wait a moment—the truth of the matter is that they never imagined men could ever become so indifferent to learning Latin, nor that a country's learning could ever become so decayed. They *deliberately* didn't bother to translate the books because they thought people who could read Latin would always be around and indeed that the general level of knowledge of Latin would actually get better, not worse!"

Then I brought to mind how the law was first found in the Hebrew language, and afterward, when the Greeks learned the law, they translated it all into their own language; and many other books as well. And af-

terward in the same way the Romans, when they had
gained this knowledge, translated it into their own
language through learned interpreters. And all other
Christian nations also translated some part of them
into their own language.

Therefore it seems essential to me—and I hope it
seems so to you, Bishop—that we should also translate
certain books that are most necessary for all men to
know, into English—the language we can all understand. We need to arrange this, as with God's help we
very easily can if we have peace, so that all the youth of
free men now among the English people, who have the
means to be able to devote themselves to study, may be
set to study (as long as they are not needed elsewhere)
until such time as they are able to read English writing
well. Afterward we can give further instruction in the
Latin language to those who wish to learn more and
who want to win promotion to holy orders.

**Then when I brought to mind how the knowledge
of Latin had previously decayed among the English
people, and yet many could read English writing, I
began amid other various and manifold cares of this
kingdom to translate into English the book which is
called *Pastoralis* in Latin and "Shepherd's Book" [i.e.,
Pastoral Care] in English, sometimes word for word,
sometimes in a paraphrase [the literal translation is
"meaning for meaning"] as I learned it from Archbishop Plegmund, and my bishop Asser, and my
priest Grimbold and my priest John.**

When I had mastered Latin as well as I could, I translated it into English as I understood it and as I could interpret it most intelligibly. And now I am sending one book to every bishopric in my kingdom; and in each there will be a bookmark worth fifty mancuses.

And in the name of God I command that no one remove the bookmark from the book nor the book from the cathedral where I send it. I don't know how long there may be such learned bishops as now, thanks be to God, there are almost everywhere; therefore I desire that the book should always reside in the cathedral, unless the bishop wants to have the book, or the book is on loan, or someone is copying from it.

Here is the original Anglo-Saxon of the passage in bold above; the one I have left in a literal translation. I have chosen this particular passage for this treatment because it lies at the very heart of what Alfred was doing.

Ða ic ða gemunde hu sio lar Lædengeðiodnes ær ðissum afeallan wæs giond Angelcynn, ond ðeah monige cuðon Englisc gewrit arædan, ða ongan ic, ongemang oðrum mislicum ond manigfaldum bisgum ðisses kynerices, ða boc wendan on Englisc ðe is genemned on Læden *Pastoralis* ond on Englisc *Hierdeboc*, hwilum word be worde, hwilum andgit be andgiete, swæ swæ ic hie geliornde æt *Plegmunde* minum ærcebiscepe ond æt *Assere* minum biscepe ond æt *Grimbolde* minum mæseprioste ond æt *Iohanne* minum mæseprioste.

At first glance, Anglo-Saxon looks very foreign, but in fact it is really simply an old-fashioned version of English and there is no need to be alarmed by it. It is true that many words in Anglo-Saxon are unfamiliar to us today (although they will be more familiar to people who have studied German or Dutch). It's also true that Anglo-Saxon uses many word-endings which modern English no longer uses and that this increases the impression of unfamiliarity.

In the above passage I provided a literal, word-by-word (as Alfred might have said) translation of the Anglo-Saxon words in bold so you can see how Anglo-Saxon works. This process of including a word-for-word translation is known as a gloss and is exactly what many Anglo-Saxon monks and scribes themselves did when they glossed a passage in Latin with words from their own everyday language—namely, Anglo-Saxon.

If my comment that Anglo-Saxon is really nothing more than an old-fashioned form of English sounds far-fetched, the best thing to do is to listen to a passage of Anglo-Saxon read aloud (recordings are available which let you hear this). Spoken Anglo-Saxon will seem more familiar and slightly more comprehensible than when written down.

Now a bit of detective work. You noticed Alfred's reference to the "bookmark" that must not be removed from the book, nor from the cathedral without incurring regal displeasure? Alfred's reference to this bookmark is particularly interesting in view of a discovery made in 1693 near

Athelney in Somerset, England. Athelney is a small village that in the past was surrounded by marshland. An object was found in the ground. It is nearly three inches long, made of filigree gold, and has a rock crystal covering. What is especially intriguing about it is that the object has a socket in the bottom in the form of an animal head. The presence of the socket suggests that the object was originally mounted on a thin rod, presumably of wood or bone.

Why should this beautiful but enigmatic object be of interest to us here? Because it's known that Alfred took refuge from the Danes in the marshes around Athelney in A.D. 878. Furthermore, under the rock crystal covering there is a rather naïve but curiously touching enameled image believed to be a "portrait" of Alfred. The portrait, held in place by a gold fret of Anglo-Saxon words, shows a man holding what looks like two rods, with an object at each end that looks like the object itself. The gold fret of words reads, in Anglo-Saxon, *Aelfred mec heht gewyrcan*, which means "Alfred ordered me to be made." (*Heht* gives us "hight," a now-obsolete word in modern English which used to mean "commanded," and is seen in some old poems.)

The object discovered in Athelney is nowadays known as the Alfred Jewel and is one of the greatest treasures of Oxford's Ashmolean Museum. Many scholars believe the Alfred Jewel to be the bookmark Alfred is referring to in the preface to his translation of *Pastoralis*. This is something that is impossible to prove, but it certainly seems likely, especially in view of the strong connection between Alfred and the place where the Jewel was found. The rods which the person in the enameled image are holding may quite possibly be the bookmarks themselves with the Jewel at the head of them.

The scholar Sir Christopher Ball is a firm believer that the Alfred Jewel is indeed the head of the bookmark mentioned in the preface to the translation of the *Pastoralis*. He also thinks that the very fact that the message on the Jewel refers to "Aelfred" and does not name him as king implies an expected *familiarity* on the part of the person likely to read the message that it was obvious who "Aelfred" was. If the person had read the preface this would indeed have been obvious, Sir Christopher maintains, so the Alfred Jewel seems all the more likely to be the bookmark Alfred mentions.

If you are ever in Oxford, it is very much worth going to see the Alfred Jewel. It doesn't look at all old-fashioned; indeed, it gives the curious impression of having been made only a day or so earlier rather than more than 1,100 years ago. It brings history alive in the sense that it reminds us that "history" was once, very simply, the present.

The question of the value of the Anglo-Saxon unit of currency known as the mancus is also interesting. In his translation Alfred says that the bookmark would be worth fifty mancuses. In the *Oxford English Dictionary*, a mancus is listed as worth "about thirty pence" but, unusually for the dictionary, it does not clarify from which period the pence are from.

In fact, Anglo-Saxon pence must be the ones referred to, as a mancus was a month's wages for a skilled worker, who would be paid a penny a day. According to the *Laws of Ine*, an important Anglo-Saxon legal code produced for the West Saxon king Ine, who reigned from A.D. 688 to 726, a mancus is worth an ox. At modern prices an ox or cow costs about £300, or about U.S. $500, but the price fluctuates widely according to market conditions. Based on this price, the bookmark would be worth about £15,000, or about U.S. $25,000, a substantial sum. No wonder Alfred was worried someone might take it from the cathedral to which it was sent.

So by the ninth century A.D., Anglo-Saxon—far from being the language of a bunch of pagan savages—was already the tongue of a people who, no matter how much they might have neglected educational matters in the struggle against the Vikings and in the general struggle for life in Anglo-Saxon Britain, were willing and able to better themselves intellectually. The language was written down very efficiently in a modified version of the Roman alphabet, and literacy rates were rising.

Is it possible that one literate Anglo-Saxon might have wondered—lying in bed late one night in his primitive but comfortable thatched cottage, with the glow of the dying fire still warming the bedroom—where exactly the letters of written Anglo-Saxon had come from? And if he (or she, for that matter) had known that the Anglo-Saxon alphabet had come from the alphabet used to write down Latin, that great language of culture, history, and religion, might not the inquisitive and thoughtful Anglo-Saxon have pondered: "All right, but then where did the Roman alphabet come from?"

Indeed, that same inquisitive Anglo-Saxon might even have wondered, just before dropping off to sleep, *where alphabets came from in the first place.*

It's a question profoundly worth answering, for how can we understand the origins of the spelling of English if we don't answer it? So let's stay awake, poke the fire, and find out.

As we've seen, the world's first comprehensive writing systems (in the sense they could be used to write down *anything* that could be said in the spoken language) were those used by the ancient Sumerians and the ancient Egyptians. Both these great cultures appear to have invented their writing systems at about the same time, around 3000 B.C., though the Sumerians may have done so a little earlier. The Sumerian writing system was known as cuneiform, which means "wedge-shaped." The word derives from the Latin *cuneous,* meaning "wedge," and refers to the fact that cuneiform was written with a wedge-shaped implement, usually in wet clay or mud, which then set hard.

It is, however, the great hieroglyphic writing system of the ancient Egyptians that is the forerunner of many of the world's alphabets, and certainly of all the alphabets currently used in Europe.

If you've seen hieroglyphs in museums or on a visit to Egypt, you'll most likely have been struck by how many hieroglyphs are stylized *pictures* of things, especially birds and animals. The ancient Greeks, who ruled in Egypt from 332 B.C. until 30 B.C., but who never actually managed to understand the Egyptians' writing system, coined the term "hieroglyph" from the Greek words *hieros,* meaning "holy," and *glyph,* meaning "carving." This is how the Greeks saw the hieroglyphs: as mystical and religious carvings.

But they weren't. Instead, they were simply a writing system. And—as you may have yourself guessed if you've ever examined a piece of hieroglyphic writing in any detail—the stylized pictures *can't* just mean the things they look like, because there are obviously too many representations of *things* for a piece of writing based around those things to make any sense, unless hieroglyphic writing consisted solely of lists of names of animals or objects, which seems unlikely.

And in fact it didn't consist of such lists, but instead was as complete and flexible a writing system as any that has ever been invented, collectively, by the human mind.

How did the hieroglyphs work? Well, to start with, some hieroglyphs *do* "mean" the thing they look like. For example, the following hieroglyphs represent:

owl   seated man   mouth   water pot

But the majority of hieroglyphs were not used in this way. Instead, they were phonograms: that is, they stood for *sounds* in the ancient Egyptian language (classical Egyptian). This is one reason why the ancient Greeks never understood how the hieroglyphic system worked, because by the time they were ruling in Egypt, the language of the ancient Egyptians was actually no longer the everyday language spoken in Egypt, and as we know, you need to understand a language if you are going to understand the writing system it uses.

In fact, many hieroglyphs that were used to write the sounds of the classical Egyptian language also meant the thing they looked like. For example, the hieroglyph used

for the *m*-sound in classical Egyptian was also the hieroglyph for "owl," shown above, which thus had in effect
two meanings, rather as if the English letter *S* were used
both to indicate the *s*-sound and also to mean "snake."
(The difference is that the word for "owl" in classical
Egyptian did not in fact begin with an *m*-sound; like most
hieroglyph phonograms, this particular hieroglyph seems
to have derived its "sound" from an even older word for
the thing represented: a word that had left the language
even before the days of classical Egyptian.)

As well as being used as logograms and phonograms,
hieroglyphs were used in other ways. In particular, some
picture-hieroglyphs were employed as *determinatives* to
give an "idea" connected to the meaning of the phrase or
sentence in question. For example, there is a hieroglyph
depicting a particular small bird, and this hieroglyph was
used to convey the idea of something worthless, presumably because the Egyptians regarded the small bird in
question as being of no worth or value.

The fact that individual hieroglyphs could be used in
a variety of ways did not, of course, make the hieroglyphic writing system any easier to decipher, and in fact
it was not finally deciphered until as late as 1822. The
decipherment—one of the greatest-ever feats of the human intellect—was achieved through a combination of
brilliant insight, inspired guesswork, good luck (the discovery of the Rosetta Stone in 1799 provided an extensive
trilingual text in Greek, demotic Egyptian, and hieroglyphic writing), and scholarly devotion (the Coptic lan-

guage used in the Coptic Church was very sensibly mastered by the principal hieroglyph decipherer Jean-François Champollion because it was the closest living relative to classical Egyptian).

But despite the multiple uses of the hieroglyphic characters, the most important and extensive way they were used was as sound symbols. They not only stood for individual phonemes, though, but often for *two* or *three* consonants. And so there were far more hieroglyphs than was strictly necessary to write down the sounds of classical Egyptian. The Egyptians had got the idea of using phonograms but they made their writing system, beautiful as it is, far more complicated than it needed to be.

The hieroglyph writing system was invented by the elite of ancient Egypt—the priests and the scribes—and it was never intended to be used by anybody else. However, there is clear archaeological evidence that by around 2000 B.C., Semitic foreign workers living in Egypt and originating mainly from countries to the east of Egypt wanted a simpler way to write things down. The hieroglyphic writing system was not something they would have known about to any detailed extent, but it appears that some of them had a smattering of knowledge about it. At any rate, they at least understood the crucial principle—so fundamental to the way the hieroglyphic writing system worked—of written symbols being used to stand for individual sounds in the Egyptian language.

Some workers saw no reason (and of course there *was* no reason) why they couldn't use as many of the hieroglyphs as they needed to write down their *own* languages. Of course, in fact they didn't need to use any hieroglyphs at all; they could simply have invented their own sound characters. All that is required for a writing system to be used is *agreement* that a certain symbol stands for something, such as a phoneme. The crucial point here is that the Semitic workers invented phoneme-by-phoneme phonograms: that is, writing systems which only need as many letters as there are phonemes (or even fewer). They created an alphabet with twenty-seven letters: the world's first.

In practice, in most cases the letters chosen by these foreign workers derived directly from hieroglyphs, which while *written* by priests and scribes were on display in places—such as temples—where foreign workers would have sometimes congregated. The workers agreed among themselves that a particular borrowed hieroglyph symbol would stand for whatever it looked like and *also* for a particular sound, just as hieroglyphs actually did in the hieroglyphic system itself.

For example, the Egyptian hieroglyph of a hand was apparently used by the foreigners to signify the word *kaph*, which meant "palm of the hand." More important, this symbol was not just used for the word *kaph* but also to indicate the *k*-sound that began the word. The Semitic foreign workers, incidentally, did not bother to write down vowel sounds, mainly because the languages they spoke relied so extensively on employing consonants to express meaning that it was perfectly possible to write these languages down without needing to specify vowel sounds. (This is not of course true of modern English.) The hieroglyphic system also did not write down vowel sounds, which explains why even the expert Egyptologists of today do not know exactly what classical Egyptian vowels sounded like, and why transliterations of hieroglyphic writing make use of approximations for writing down vowels.

This inspired borrowing by foreign workers of the writing principle at the heart of the Egyptian hieroglyphs led directly to the evolution of the Phoenician alphabet, which had developed by about 1000 B.C.

The Phoenicians were an efficient and practical Iron Age people, based in what is now Lebanon. Today they are justly remembered as the most effective and skilled seafarers of the ancient world. They were enthusiastic traders and merchants; from about 700 B.C. they started building a seaborne trade network around the Mediterranean, for example exchanging North African elephant tusks for bars of silver or tin from Spain.

What makes their alphabet exciting is that a clear line of descent can be traced from it down to the Roman alphabet and by extension to the alphabet of modern English. Indeed, according to David Sacks, whose excellent book *The Alphabet* is essential reading if you want to know more about this subject, "About nineteen of our letters can be traced back directly—in their shapes, their alphabetical sequence, and, for most, their sounds—to Phoenician counterparts."

By around 1000 B.C., the Phoenicians were writing down their language in a twenty-two-letter alphabet. Like the hieroglyphic and Semitic systems it evolved from, the Phoenician alphabet got by without using letters for vowels. For instance, their written *a*- and *e*-sounds are not actual vowel sounds but, respectively, a breathing stop and a shout of surprise. But the lack of vowel sounds in their alphabet did not matter to them, because the nature of their language meant that an array of consonants was sufficient to give enough information to make clear what word was being written down, while occasional ambiguities could be handled by looking at the words in context.

The Phoenician alphabet was in many respects the grandfather of every alphabet used in Europe today. In particular, it was the ancestor of the Greek alphabet, which unlike its Phoenician counterpart *did* use vowel sounds. The Greek alphabet, which appears to have first been developed sometime around 900 B.C., made use of consonant and vowel sounds, and by about 200 B.C. its classical form was established. Even great civilizations try to minimize the work involved in any invention and are happy to borrow ideas from the past, and this explains why the ancient Greeks and Romans so readily borrowed alphabet letters. As Greek and Latin use more or less the same phonemes, there was not a particular need for the Romans to invent a completely new alphabet, but they adapted the Greek alphabet to their own requirements.

It's time to look at the evolution of all the letters, not

only of the Roman and Anglo-Saxon alphabets, but also of the modern English alphabet.

— A —

The evolution of the letter A can be traced very precisely from a pictogram of an ox's head, which was simplified in early Semitic inscriptions into this:

This evolved into the Phoenician letter *aleph*, which in turn resulted in the Greek A (or *alpha*) that is the ancestor of our own A.

Did the high value of an ox to Iron Age people make it a perfect candidate on which to base the first letter of the alphabet? We cannot know for certain, but this certainly seems possible.

— B —

The letter B is derived from the hieroglyph for "reed shelter":

This probably inspired the Semitic workers, living in Egypt, to invent a letter they called "house" in their language, or—as the word actually was—*bayt*. The Phoenician letter B is starting to look a little like our own B.

Later developments reversed the Phoenician letter and closed the space between the "tail" and the main body of the letter.

— C —

C derived from a Phoenician letter known as *gimel*, which looked like this:

The letter's name probably meant a hunter's "throwing stick": that is, a sharpened spear with a handle that would allow it to be thrown. By the time of the Greeks, this letter had evolved into the letter *gamma*, which is really already the familiar C.

— D —

The Phoenician letter from which D derives was, appropriately enough, door-shaped and did indeed mean "door."

The Phoenician word *dalet* began with a *d*-sound, and the letter has never lost this sound as it evolved through the Greek and Roman alphabets into the letter we know today.

— E —

The letter E started life as a Semitic pictogram dating from about 1800 B.C.

This was, clearly, a person. It is believed that it was a picture of a person who was crying out. The letter was known as *he* by the Phoenicians: not a reference to the sex of the person but perhaps a reference to the cry, which (as David Sacks shrewdly points out) is like our "Hey!" As the pictogram evolved into a letter, it continued to represent the *h*-sound. It was only around 725 B.C. that the Greeks assigned this letter the vowel sound of *e*. By that point the letter looked like this:

Later the letter was reversed by the Romans so that it started to resemble the letter E of today—this was usually caused by a switch from writing right to left to writing left to right.

— **F** —

The letter F has a complex pedigree. It started out as a Phoenician letter which looked like this, but took the *w*-sound:

The Greeks later adapted this letter into the following letter, which they first called *wau* and later *digamma*:

Later still the letter went through the familiar reversal process, but it was only the Romans, around 200 B.C., who gave the letter its straight lines and, most important, started to use it to represent the *f*-sound.

— G —

G was essentially an invention of the Romans, though it was probably based on the Greek letter *zeta*. G dates from about 250 B.C., when it looked very much as it looks today:

G

— H —

The letter H started life as a Phoenician pictogram, *khet*, that meant "a fence" and was pronounced with a hard *ch*-sound at the start, a bit like clearing one's throat, and looked like this:

The shape of the pictogram evolved until, by as early as 400 B.C., it was identical to our H of today.

— **I** —

The letter I derives from the Phoenician pictogram *yod*, which meant "arm and hand." It took the *y*-sound as in the word "year." It looked like this:

The pictogram gradually evolved into a simple stick-shaped letter that was used by the Romans to spell both the short *i*-sound (as in "ship") and the longer sound as in "sheep." Even by the twelfth century A.D., the letter was still used in English to spell the short *i*-sound, the sound of the pronoun "I," and also the *y*-sound in "year," as before. In modern English the letter can be used for a wide variety of sounds, except for the *y*-sound in "year," for which English nowadays prefers the letter Y.

— **J** —

The Roman alphabet had no letter J because very early Latin did not have the *y*-sound in "year." When this sound began to appear it was represented by the letter I, as in Latin words such as *ius* ("law"). Throughout the Anglo-Saxon period, the letter I did service for the *y*-sound in "year." This sound was mainly used in Anglo-Saxon for writing names of Romance origin that began with this *y*-sound. In Britain, it was only in about A.D.

1500, under the influence of printing, that printers found it useful finally to distinguish between the letter I used as a vowel and the letter I used to spell the *y*-sound in "year." They added a little tail to the letter I and produced a J. In English today, the letter J is no longer used to spell the *y*-sound in "year": The letter Y is always preferred. However, in many European languages the J is pronounced like an English Y.

— K—

As we have seen, the letter K ultimately derives from an Egyptian hieroglyph, as most Roman letters do:

This hieroglyph apparently inspired the Semitic foreigners in Egypt to invent a symbol for "hand," which actually meant "palm of the hand" and was pronounced as *kaph*:

This symbol eventually evolved into the Greek letter *kappa*, which looks like our familiar K in reverse. *Kappa* did not, however, mean "hand" and had no meaning apart from being the name of the letter. The letter was later reversed.

Generally, alphabets whose letters have the luxury of not needing to do service as a picture of something evolved *after* alphabets whose letters *did* mean something. Of course, the sounds of the names of some letters in the English alphabet do have other meanings, but that is a co-incidence; the only meaning of the actual letters is themselves.

— L —

The letter L comes from the Greek letter *lambda*, which originally looked like a reversed version of an uppercase L. The earlier origins of *lambda* are not certain, but it probably did have a Semitic origin. The English letter L was already essentially finalized by around 200 B.C., when the Roman L began to attain the right-angled shape familiar to us, with the bottom line to the right of the vertical line.

— M —

This letter originated from the Egyptian hieroglyph that meant "water"—and in fact had the *m*-sound:

The hieroglyph evolved into a similarly shaped symbol called *mem*, which meant "water" in the language of the

Semitic foreigners. By about 725 B.C. this letter had changed into the Greek letter *mu*:

Under the Romans, *mu* became more upright and regularly shaped, giving the Roman M, which is essentially identical to our own.

— N —

It will hardly surprise us that, snakes being so much a part of the world of the ancient Egyptians, there was a snake hieroglyph:

The snake hieroglyph was borrowed by the Semitic foreign workers to make a letter that was part of their twenty-seven-letter alphabet. This letter originally took an *n*-sound, though the reason for this is more complex than one would imagine. The word for "snake" in the Semitic workers' language was *nahash*, but for the letter's name we must rely on some sources in which it is known as *nun*, meaning "fish." In any event, both words began with an *n*-sound. By about 740 B.C., the Greeks had developed a letter they called *nu*, whose name, shape, sound, and even position in the alphabet they borrowed from the Phoenicians, who themselves must have borrowed it from the Semitic workers. Our own letter N comes directly from *nu,* via—as usual—the Romans.

— O —

The letter O was very much the way it is today as far back as 725 B.C., when the letter the Greeks called *omicron* (meaning "little o") was already looking exactly like the letter we know today.

The evolutionary process here followed the usual pattern of Egyptian hieroglyphs→Semitic workers→ Phoenicians→Greeks→Romans. The original hieroglyph that was the ancestor of our modern O was the hieroglyph for "eye":

It inspired a Semitic letter *ayin,* which meant "eye" and looked like this:

By the time of the Phoenicians, the diagrammatic drawing of an eye had simplified into a circle, and the rest is history.

— P —

The origins of the letter P can be traced back to the Semitic letter *pe*, which meant "mouth" and looked approximately like one:

The shape of the letter underwent considerable changes, including, most famously of all, the Greek letter π (*pi*) which represented a *p*-sound and is also an important mathematical symbol today (representing the ratio of the circumference of a circle to its diameter). However, there was also a Greek letter P, or *rho*, which had an *r*-sound (and still does in the modern Greek alphabet and in the Cyrillic alphabet) but which has a different line of descent, discussed below. The original letter that meant "mouth" was probably the ancestor of the Greek P. The Romans did not bother with a P but simply borrowed the Greek P, or *rho*, to stand for the sound that the Greek P had represented. English has borrowed this letter, and its sound, from the Romans.

— Q —

An unusual letter in modern English—owing to the fact that in words of purely English origin it is always followed by a U—Q can be traced back to the Phoenician letter *qoph*, which meant "monkey":

Admittedly, this does not look much like a monkey. Very likely the Phoenician letter derived from an earlier letter that was more monkeylike, but no such letter has been discovered to date. As the letter evolved into our modern Q, it went through various incarnations, all of which retain the idea of the letter being essentially an O with a tail. By the time of the Romans, the letter had attained its modern form. The letter combination *qu* was very important in Latin: Many common words began with it. Today, there are dozens of words in English that derive from Latin words which began with *qu* and which we often spell very much as the Romans spelled them.

—R—

This letter has its origins in the Semitic letter *resh*, which meant "head" and looked like the outline of one:

By the time of the Greeks, as the result of several evolutionary changes that included a switch from the letter facing left to facing right, the letter had developed into Greek *rho*, which looked exactly like a modern P but was pronounced with an *r*-sound. However, when the Romans borrowed *rho* they needed to distinguish it from their letter P (their form for the Greek *pi*), so they added a "tail" to it to produce R. Our own R is very simply borrowed from theirs.

— S —

Considering that the shape of S seems so simple, the letter has undergone some significant shape changes since its earliest days. It started life as a letter that looked like an archer's bow and dates from about 1750 B.C.:

The name and precise sound of this letter remain unknown. By the time of the Phoenicians, the "archer's bow" letter had evolved into a letter the Phoenicians called *shin*:

W

This obviously looks like a W and nothing like an S. However, in early Greek writing the Phoenician letter was changed into an upright zigzag, and then the letter underwent a process of reversal when it was borrowed by the Romans. Under them, the S acquired the shape it has today.

It is worth noting that by the early Middle Ages in Britain, an additional way of writing a lowercase *s* developed. It was written like an F but without the horizontal stroke, and was used only at the start or middle of the word, never at the end. This way of writing *s* became popular with printers in the late fifteenth century, but by the nineteenth century it had fallen out of fashion. Like the Y thorn, it can still be seen on old gravestones.

—T—

Of all the letters used in the English alphabet today, T and X have been been least subject to change over the years. This is no doubt because of their very fundamental shape, which of course is also the shape of the cross in the Christian faith.

The Semitic alphabet, the Phoenician alphabet, and the Greek alphabet all featured a T that looks essentially like the T we use today. Sometimes the letter was written with the horizontal line at the very top (as in the uppercase T of the modern alphabet and other languages that use the Roman alphabet) and sometimes with some of the vertical line left above the horizontal line (as in the lowercase *t*). But it was the same letter, and is easily readable by us today even though it was first written down close to 3,000 years ago. The letter has had the *t*-sound since at least 800 B.C., when it was used by the Phoenicians to represent that sound.

— U and V —

These letters should be treated together because they both had a common origin and for most of their history were, in fact, used interchangeably. The first identifiable ancestor of these letters is the Phoenician letter *waw*, which came sixth in their alphabet and took a *w*-sound:

The Greeks called this letter *upsilon* when they adapted it into their alphabet in about 700 B.C. However, the Etruscans, who like the Romans lived on the Italian peninsula, dropped the bottom vertical line of the letter, so that it wound up looking like a V. In fact, the Romans would often write the *u*-sound as a V, but careless writing led to the letter having a more rounded bottom so that it looked more like the U of today, and the Romans eventually tended to use V and U fairly interchangeably, partly because straight lines are easier to carve than round ones and Latin was frequently carved into stone. This procedure was copied when the Roman alphabet was borrowed to write down English. Even by the time Shakespeare's plays were printed in the early sixteenth century, the two letters were still being used interchangeably, although V was usually preferred for the start of a word. It was only by about A.D. 1700 that the custom of using the sharp-bottomed V to mean the consonant sound and the curve-bottomed U to mean the vowel sound began to arise, and even then it was more than a century later before a clear and decisive separation between U and V was achieved. As late as 1836, in the *New Dictionary of the English Language,* the entry for "udder" comes after "vaunt" and before "veal," which suggests that even then the letters U and V were felt to be basically the same.

— W —

The *w*-sound is known technically as a voiced bilabial semivowel—a *voiced bilabial* because we need our vocal cords and lips to say it, and a *semivowel* because it functions as a consonant but lacks the decisive sound of one.

The Romans represented the *w*-sound by using two of their V letters, or two of their U letters. Later, the Anglo-Saxons preferred—as we have seen—to use their runic letter *wyn* to depict the *w*-sound. However, the Norman invasion displaced the use of *wyn* in favor of the use of the Roman "double U," which is still what we call the letter W even though nowadays we write it, ironically, as basically a joined-up double letter V.

— X —

X derives from the letter *ksi* (or *xi*) of the Greek alphabet, which looks very much like the letter we use in the English alphabet today. It is not known precisely how the letter came into Greek, but the simplicity and pleasing symmetry of its shape make it an obvious shape for any letter, and it is difficult to believe that the Greeks invented it.

X was originally the last letter of the Roman alphabet and represented the same sound it represents in English now, the *ks* consonant sound in words such as "rex" and "exit," which were both Latin words in the past and are English words today. By about A.D. 100 two additional letters to the Roman alphabet—Y and Z—were put at the end so that X was no longer the last letter. Our own X was a direct borrowing from the Romans.

—Y—

The ancient Greek letter *upsilon,* which we have already encountered, became the ancestor of the English letter Y. The Romans called it by the same name as the Greeks did, although they wrote it differently, because the Greek alphabet, while it lent many letters to the Roman alphabet, was far from identical to it. In Latin, the letter took a vowel sound; today it is used in English both as a vowel sound (such as in "my") and as a semivowel (such as in "year").

—Z—

This letter derives ultimately from the Phoenician letter *zayin*, meaning "the axe" (or "ax"), which took a *z*-sound and looked like this:

I

The direct descendant of *zayin* was the Greek letter *zeta*, which originally (in about 700 B.C.) closely resembled its Phoenician ancestor but which later, by about 400 B.C., had acquired the familiar Z shape. The letter was borrowed from the Greeks by the Romans and subsequently from the Romans by the Anglo-Saxons. However, there has always been a tradition in English that Z, representing a sound that is not very common in English, is a fairly unimportant letter. In Shakespeare's *King Lear*, written in about 1605, the Earl of Kent at one point berates the fawning servant of one of his enemies with the insult "thou whoreson zed, thou unnecessary letter!"

Whatever you think about the zed (or "zee," as it is called in America), it is an essential part of the alphabet. It is also a high point-scorer in Scrabble, if you are that way inclined.

What conclusions, finally, should we be drawing about the ultimate value of the principle of the alphabet?

All writing systems have their particular virtues and drawbacks. As I suggested at the start of the previous chapter, we shouldn't single out the alphabet principle for inherent special praise just because it happens to be the system used for writing down English.

Still, if a language is written down in a more or less phonetic way, the crucial fact that alphabets never use more than about thirty letters makes any alphabetic writing system far easier to learn than a logographic system. Chinese, for example, being composed of logographic characters that each represent a unit of meaning, has many thousands of characters that must be learned. At least 4,000 must be mastered to gain a reasonable competence in writing everyday Chinese, and real literacy requires a writer to know about 10,000 characters: a daunting task even for native Chinese speakers.

In addition, an alphabetic writing system is always going to offer the extremely useful benefit of providing guidance to readers on how a word should be *pronounced*. After all, the letters of the alphabet are designed to do precisely that. Even in English—such a woefully unphonetic language—the alphabet does give *some* guidance to how unfamiliar words should be pronounced.

We have now traced the origins of our modern alphabet and explored some of the ways in which the alphabet scores over other writing systems. Let's now take a look at the ways these letters come together to form the basis for why English spelling is the way it is.

Part Three

Why English Spelling Is the Way It Is

Chapter 5

———

Before English Existed

What we do in life echoes in eternity.

> —Maximus the gladiator, in *Gladiator* (2000);
> screenplay by David Franzoni, John Logan,
> and William Nicholson

HE story of English spelling is an improbable one in every sense. It is a tale of a process of evolution that contains so many curious accidents and bizarre twists of fate that the end result—how we spell English today—must be regarded as one of the most absurd, ridiculous, and protracted (1,500 years and counting) accidents of human culture.

Yet no matter how accidental and ridiculous the story of English spelling is, and no matter how many suggestions have been made for "improving" English spelling (which is normally taken to mean making it more consistent), the ridiculous accident of English spelling has continued on its merry path much as before, and it's the would-be reformers who have, largely, been forgotten.

As our glance at Anglo-Saxon in the previous chapter

suggested, the story of English spelling is, inevitably, intimately bound up with the story of the language itself. We have so far looked at what writing and spelling actually are, how they work, what alphabets are and where they come from. These subjects are all, in their own way, part of the improbable story of English spelling. But it's time now to move from the general to the particular, and look at how English spelling evolved from its very earliest days.

Because writing is so intimately bound up with language, investigating how English *uses* its alphabet means looking at where the English language itself came from. So let's go back to the very earliest days in the story of English. Days, in fact, that were *so* early, English didn't even exist.

The English language belongs to the major language family known as Indo-European. Indo-European is one of the world's most important language families in terms of the number of modern languages that belong to it and the number of people who speak them.

The Indo-European language family includes a wide range of tongues that are—or have been—spoken in a region that originally ranged from Iceland in the west to India in the east. Today, substantially because of the commercial and political success of the European nations, Indo-European languages—especially English—are spoken all around the world.

Within the language family of Indo-European there are a number of branches, each of which contains various languages that all share many similar characteristics and often have similar words for the same thing. Scholars have identified a total of ten branches of the Indo-European language family. These branches are as follows, listed in order of the age of the oldest significant writings of any language in the group, with the oldest first:

* Anatolian
* Indo-Iranian
* Greek
* Italic
* Germanic
* Armenian
* Tocharian
* Celtic
* Balto-Slavic
* Albanian

The very fact that there is an Indo-European language family presupposes that there was once a parent language, called by scholars for convenience Proto-Indo-European (and often abbreviated to PIE), which was *the ancestor of every Indo-European language*. PIE was spoken in the days—probably about 5,000 years ago—before the various branches of Indo-European started to diverge. This divergence happened because the various tribes who originally spoke PIE began to move to different parts of Europe and

India. As they became more and more geographically separated, the languages they spoke began to differ from the original PIE, and gradually constituted new languages that gave birth to new branches of the Indo-European language family.

PIE itself must have been spoken before the geographical separation of Indo-European tribes started. There is no way of knowing how old PIE itself is, which is another way of saying that we know nothing whatsoever for certain about the language from which PIE derived. The general view of scholars, however, is that language was something that developed in several parts of the world, so we can't assume that if we go back far enough we will find one original language from which all the 6,800 living languages of today's world originated.

As far as is known, nothing survives that was written in PIE, and indeed there's no actual evidence that PIE was ever written down at all. Yet quite a bit of information about the language has been pieced together by scholars, mainly by carefully extrapolating developments in known languages that are descendants of the original language and undertaking a kind of "reverse engineering" to arrive at a likely earlier stage of development of these known languages. This earlier stage is referred to as PIE. There isn't a complete and unified knowledge of this original language, but a surprising amount is known about it.

How did the idea that PIE might have existed *at all* first get put forward? Curiously, the idea was one of the more positive aspects of colonialism, for it stemmed directly from British administrators going to India in the eighteenth century, during the early days of the British Empire.

Many of these administrators had been educated at English private schools, where the study of Latin and classical Greek formed a central part of the syllabus. Once they reached India, the administrators often got to know something of the Sanskrit language, which was spoken in India at about the same time Latin and classical Greek were being spoken in Europe.

Just as Latin is the ancestor of modern Romance languages such as Italian, French, Spanish, Portuguese, and so on, and classical Greek is the ancestor of modern Greek, Sanskrit is the ancestor of modern Indian languages such as Hindi, Bengali, Nepali, and Sinhalese. Today, however, Sanskrit is not as dead as Latin and classical Greek are. A form of Sanskrit is used even nowadays, in the twenty-first century, as a medium for learned communication between Hindu scholars, and by some scholars as a language for original writing.

When the British administrators got to know Sanskrit, they were astonished by numerous obviously close resemblances between many Sanskrit words and Latin and Greek words.

For example, the Sanskrit words for "father," "mother," and "brother" are, respectively, *pitar, matar,* and *bhratar,* whereas the corresponding Latin words are *pater, mater,* and *frater* and the Greek words are *pater, meter,* and *phrater.* To take another example, the word for "three" is *trayas* in Sanskrit, *treis* in Greek, and *tres* in Latin.

These and many other similarities drew the foreign administrators to the irresistible conclusion that there was only one possible explanation why these three languages from such diverse geographic regions could have such similar vocabulary. What other explanation could there be but that the three languages were *themselves* all descendants of an even older language that had been spoken in the past but was now extinct?

And this was, in fact, exactly what had happened. And that language was Proto-Indo-European.

By careful and painstaking work, scholars specializing in comparative linguistics have been able to work out what the main sounds of PIE really were. They also know a good deal about the grammar of the language. As far as actual PIE *words* are concerned, in the absence of any written record of PIE there can be no definite knowledge of this, but the process of backward extrapolation has revealed, fairly reliably, what a few dozen words in PIE *probably* sounded like. Here are some examples. Because there is no standardized spelling of PIE words, the PIE spellings I use here are attempts to write the phonetic sounds of Indo-European in English letters:

kwon   "dog" (This is where the Latin word for "dog," *canis*—which gives us our word "canine"—

ultimately comes from; or rather, this is the very first known form of the word.)

ekwo	"horse"
ewi	"sheep" (This word is an ancestor of the English word "ewe.")
gow	"cow"
su	"pig"
wogho	"vehicle"
yugo	"yoke"
medhu	This was an alcoholic drink, probably like mead, and the very word "mead" is related to it.
kuningaz	"king"

Intriguing proof that the PIE word for "king" was indeed almost certainly *kuningaz* is seen in the fact that the *modern* Finnish word for "king" is *kuningas*. Scholars believe that the Indo-European word was borrowed several thousand years ago by Finns engaged on trading missions to central or southern Europe, and that Finland's comparative geographic isolation led to the loanword being preserved intact.

The particular branch of Indo-European to which English belongs is *Germanic*. In fact, for reasons we'll examine, modern English has a strong French element to it as well as its basic Germanic element. But French belongs to another regional language group—the *Italic* branch that was to produce Latin and, later, French itself. However, English must be allocated to the Germanic branch, because in its earliest form it was *entirely* a Germanic language.

The Germanic language branch itself is usually divided into three regional groups: East Germanic, North Germanic, and West Germanic.

The languages of the East Germanic group, which include the languages known as Burgundian, Vandal, and various dialects of the Gothic language, are all now extinct. In general, little is known about East Germanic languages, but there is one exception. By a quirk of fate, stemming from the devout religious passion of one particular Goth named Ulfilas, a good deal *is* known about one particular Gothic dialect. This is the dialect known as Visigothic, spoken along the western shore of the Black Sea (modern Romania, Bulgaria, and Turkey) in the fourth century A.D. It's worth taking a look at this dialect, because it reveals much about the people who spoke it: people who are *the oldest definitely known linguistic ancestors of anyone who speaks and writes English*.

History has not been particularly kind to the Goths. They have gone down in the annals as the invaders and destroyers of ancient Rome. The name "Goth" has rarely been used in a complimentary sense. Modern teenagers who regard themselves as adhering to "Goth" fashion and style dress in black, listen to sinister music about premature death, and think dark thoughts in the comfort of their bedrooms. As for the Vandals—the name of one of the tribes with whom the Goths eventually went southward to deal with Rome—their name has given the English language a word meaning anyone who causes violent, wanton destruction.

Ridley Scott's movie *Gladiator* (2000) depicts the Goths in cahoots with other Germanic tribes as the enemy in the battle scene that starts the movie and which is set toward the end of the second century A.D. (This powerful, primeval battle scene looks as if it were filmed in some dark, sinister Gothic forest, but was actually filmed a few miles from the M25 motorway in the southern British county of Surrey.) The Goths are portrayed as ruthless savages. The Romans send a negotiator on horseback to discuss peace terms with the Goths, who respond diplomatically by sending the negotiator back to the Roman lines minus his head.

Not, it would seem, very pleasant people.

But there was much more to the Goths than this. In fact, it was one of their number who was responsible for the first extensive writing ever done in a Germanic language.

Ulfilas—this is his Latin name; he was known as Wulfila in Gothic—was a Christian bishop and missionary who was born in or around A.D. 311. He most likely died in A.D. 382, apparently in Constantinople, which is now known as Istanbul. Knowledge of the Visigothic dialect is derived primarily from the remains of a translation of the Greek Bible he made for the Visigoths living along the river Danube.

A devout, highly educated man with high-ranking political connections, Ulfilas decided he would devote himself to translating the Bible (from Greek rather than Latin) into the everyday Gothic spoken by himself and his people. The surviving manuscripts of this translation are not originals but copies believed to have been written in northern Italy during the period of Ostrogothic rule (A.D. 493–554). The manuscripts include large portions of the New Testament.

The most extensive manuscript for providing evidence of the Visigothic language is known today as the Codex Argenteus and is housed in the library of Uppsala University in Sweden. It is a splendid manuscript, written in silver and gold letters on purple parchment. Ulfilas is believed to have translated the entire Bible into Gothic, except for the Book of Kings, but only portions of the four Gospels have survived (in 188 pages remaining out of an original estimated 330 to 336). However, they are extensive enough to provide comprehensive information about the Gothic language.

Ulfilas unquestionably deserves to be seen as one of the heroes of the story of writing. His people were fond of war, and were never so happy as when they were conquering land that didn't actually belong to them. But, at least when not lopping negotiators' heads off, they were not savages. They were a cultured and religious people who spent much of their leisure time concerned about complex issues of theology and religious belief.

It is possible that East Germanic languages already had a written form, as a few ancient runes have been discovered that appear to be attempts to write down some East Germanic languages. But the first unquestionable and extensive evidence for the writing of any East Germanic language only appears when Ulfilas comes onto the scene.

In order to carry out the remarkable feat of setting down the Visigothic dialect, Ulfilas had first to perform the far from trivial task of actually inventing a Gothic alphabet. This is one of the few occasions in the history of writing when the invention of a particular alphabet can be traced to just one person.

Through the magic of writing, Ulfilas gave his people the priceless benefit of a writing system, and access to the most holy book they knew, in their own language. Admittedly, they had to learn to read in order to appreciate the gift, but at least Ulfilas had created the possibility for them to enjoy it. His invention of a Gothic alphabet and his biblical translation led directly to the creation of a national Gothic church which made use of written Gothic. Unfortunately, however, apart from the Gothic Bible extracts, little other evidence of written Gothic has survived to modern times.

Here are the letters of the Gothic alphabet Ulfilas invented so he could write a translation of the Bible. He created his alphabet mainly from Greek letters, but he also seems to have adapted a few symbols from Latin.

𐌰	*a*	𐌾	*j*
𐌱	*b*	𐌿	*u*
𐌲	*g*	𐍀	*p*
𐌳	*d*	𐍂	*r*
𐌴	*e*	𐍃	*s*
𐌵	*q*	𐍄	*t*
𐌶	*z*	𐍅	*w*
𐌷	*h*	𐍆	*f*
𐌸	*th*	𐍇	*x*
𐌹	*i*	𐍈	*hw*
𐌺	*k*	𐍉	*o*
𐌻	*l*		
𐌼	*m*	𐍁	*90*
𐌽	*n*	𐍊	*900*

Ulfilas's extraordinary achievement is even more remarkable if we reflect that he had to deal with inventing not only an alphabet for his work, but also many new Gothic words. There simply did not exist Gothic words for many of the biblical terms and concepts. He therefore extended the Gothic vocabulary in three main ways.

First, by using existing Gothic words but giving them a new meaning. For example, the existing Gothic word *galga*, which meant "pole," gained the meaning of "cross"—a word obviously essential for any translation of the Bible. Second, he created new compounds and derivatives. For example, he was obliged to invent a word to translate the Greek word for "altar." He did this by creating a new

Gothic compound *hunslastaψs,* meaning "place of sacrifice." The Gothic letter ψ only covered the voiceless pronunciation of the *th* in "thin." Apart from this letter, the letters of Gothic have been anglicized in these examples for clarity. Third, Ulfilas borrowed some Greek and Latin words, adopting them into Gothic spelling. For example, he borrowed the Greek word *prophetes* for "prophet" and made it *praufetus* in Gothic.

The great significance of Ulfilas's work is that, following his invention of the Gothic alphabet, writing could be used for the first time ever in the Germanic world for the propagation of ideas. In a very real sense, every time we write English, we are continuing a tradition that Ulfilas started. His name deserves to be much better known.

And many Gothic words look curiously familiar, as if our own versions of them are half-remembered echoes of our ancient Germanic past that is not, perhaps, quite as ancient as we might imagine. Here are some common Gothic words and their modern English equivalents:

airψ   "earth"
barn   "child" (a wonderful distant echo of the word "bairn," which is found both in Scots dialect and in northern England. This comes from the North Germanic word *barn,* which is itself connected, historically, with the Gothic word.)
briggan   "bring"
dags   "day"

dragk	"drank"
fisks	"fish"
fugls	"bird" (There is a connection here with the modern English word "fowl.")
hlaiban	"loaf" or "bread"
hunds	"dog"
sitan	"to sit"
slepan	"to sleep"
stains	"stone"
ψank	"thanks"
tunψus	"tooth"
windan	"wind"
wulfs	"wolf"

Another Gothic word, *wairpan*, "to throw," is connected with the modern English word "warp," which means the threads "thrown" lengthways across a loom. Another interesting connection is an old dialect word of the English Midlands, "mouldwarp," which means "mole." This was a reference to the animal's habit of throwing earth—for which "mould" was an old word—behind it when it digs its holes. And remember the Icelandic word *sjónvarp*, which we came across earlier in this book, and how it means "picture-thrower," or a television?

It is fascinating to reflect that a Goth from the fourth century A.D., visiting any country today where English is spoken, would at least be able to understand some of the words used there.

What happened to the Goths? Well, later in their history, seeking warmer climates, they moved south with various other Germanic tribes and conquered much of Italy and Spain. Once they had settled in their new warm homes, they did what most Americans who move south to Mexico *don't* tend to do. That is, the Goths seemed on the whole happy to forgo their own language and adopt the language of the people whose countries they invaded.

I have never quite understood why, when the Goths and other Germanic tribes moved south and took over the Roman Empire, they didn't keep their own language and discard Latin. Had they done this, Latin would be as obscure today as Gothic now is, and the modern languages of Italy, France, Spain, Portugal, and Romania would be descendants of Gothic rather than Latin.

So why didn't this happen? If we recall the fate of the culture of the Franks when they moved into Gaul, we will probably conclude that something similar occurred when the Goths took over Rome itself.

In fact, in the past it wasn't that unusual for conquerors eventually to adopt the language, customs, and culture of the people they occupied. This was especially the case if the language, customs, and culture of the occupied people were regarded as high status and attractive, which would have very much applied when the Goths took over Rome. We also need to remember that in the past—and certainly in the fourth century A.D.—the poor quality of physical communications meant it was close to impossible for conquerors to keep up regular contact with the homeland they and their language and culture originally came from. It is only in much more recent centuries that conquerors have been able to keep in close contact with where they originated.

In the case of the Goths, my guess is that when they conquered Rome and took over what was left of the Roman Empire, they couldn't believe their luck. They came from settlements where the architecture was pretty basic, and suddenly they owned one of the greatest cities on earth! Of course, they were proud of their own culture, but as they settled in as masters of their new environment they enjoyed the Roman culture and way of life (and the wine, of course). The fact that they would probably have seen the Roman church as closer to the heart and essence of Christianity than theirs would have helped. And I imagine they would have found the Romans attractive, too, and readily intermarried with them. I'm not suggesting the Gothic language would have been discarded overnight, but it's not difficult to understand why, far from their homeland and with no plans to return anyway, the new Gothic masters of Rome—and of course their children— would have soon become Latin speakers.

In any event, the Gothic language seems to have been abandoned within a century or so after the Goths went south, though the time frame within which this happened is not precisely known.

At the same time, the numbers of Goths "back home" who spoke Gothic started to dwindle, mainly because of assimilation by neighboring peoples. Gothic did persist for a while longer, but mainly as the language of the liturgy of the Gothic church.

By the ninth century Gothic was still being used in some churches near the lower Danube. However, after that the language—the oldest known ancestor of English—only survived among a small community of Goths in the Crimean region. This community was last mentioned in the middle of the sixteenth century by a distinguished Flemish diplomat, linguist, and scholar with the easy-to-spell name of Augier Ghislain de Busbecq, who was incidentally the man who discovered the tulip in Turkey in 1551 and in 1562 arranged for a cargo of tulip bulbs to be sent from Turkey to Antwerp in Belgium and thereby created Europe's craze for tulips.

When de Busbecq wasn't being charmed by flowers, he took a deep interest in the local people of the countries he visited. A highly intelligent and able man, he was well aware how interesting it was that a community thought to have vanished did in fact still exist, so between 1560 and 1562 he collected a number of words and phrases from the Goths he met in the Crimea.

De Busbecq wrote up his research in a short and fascinating paper, which, as an educated man, he composed in Latin—the language of learning and education in the sixteenth century. Being Germanic in origin, some of the language of the Crimean Goths was evidently similar to the Flemish that was de Busbecq's mother tongue, but there were plenty of other words that were characteristically Gothic rather than Flemish.

De Busbecq's spellings are inevitably only approximations, but there is no doubt the Crimean Goths were
speaking a language that was still essentially a form of
Gothic. To take just two examples: They used the word
baar to mean "boy" (in fact, they may have said *baan*, and
de Busbecq, or his printer, might have misspelled it), and
they used the word *iel* to mean "healthy," which was close
to that of the word *hails* for "healthy" in the biblical translation of Ulfilas.

There is, unfortunately, no further mention of the
Crimean Gothic community after the sixteenth century,
and the only assumption can be that they were assimilated
by local populations.

But *did* Gothic completely vanish? The late Professor
C. L. Wrenn, a distinguished scholar who was the tutor of
Anglo-Saxon expert Sir Christopher Ball at Oxford in the
1950s, believed it possible that some remote enclave—a
village here or there, perhaps—in what was then the Soviet
Union might have survived where Gothic, or at least a
form of it, was still spoken. Wrenn even talked about leading an expedition to try to find such a village, but the political situation in the Soviet Union in the 1950s was
hardly ideal for allowing such a trip.

While the notion of Gothic having survived may seem
a little too romantic and far-fetched to be plausible,
Christopher Ball told me he thinks it "certainly possible"
that some Gothic words, at least, may have survived in dialects spoken in remote villages in the Crimea even today.
And perhaps this is indeed the case. If so, it would be fas-

cinating if one day some evidence materialized—just as the original Proto-Indo-European word *kuningas* is still used on the streets of modern Finland.

The other two branches of regional Germanic include many modern languages.

North Germanic includes, among living languages, Danish, Norwegian, Swedish, Faeroese (the language of the Faroe islands), and Icelandic.

West Germanic includes German, Dutch, Afrikaans, Flemish (which is basically a slight variant of Dutch spoken in Belgium), and Frisian. The other member of the West Germanic language family is English itself.

All the Germanic languages—East Germanic, North Germanic, and West Germanic—are relatives of English, with Gothic being, as we've seen, the oldest relative about whom a significant amount is known. Gothic is, so to speak, the great-great-grandfather who dandles modern English on his lap at a family reunion.

But while many of the other people at the family reunion share some features with the baby, including most of the other children who are also present, nobody else actually looks *a lot* like English. Frisian, spoken by the inhabitants of islands in the North Sea off the Dutch and German coast, is regarded by linguists as the language most closely related to English. If you go to the Frisian islands and listen to the language spoken there, you'll sometimes momentarily think you're hearing English spoken.

But the illusion does not last longer than a moment; the truth is that English and Frisian are really quite different.

Many of the other babies resemble each other very closely. Norwegian and Swedish, for example, are so intimately related that in some respects it could be said they are regarded as different languages more for historical and political reasons rather than for linguistic ones. Danish is also closely related to them. As for Dutch and German, they are reasonably close relatives, but more when spoken than written down, because the German and Dutch spelling systems are quite different.

Of course, English and German have many similarities, which is hardly surprising as Germans are really only English people who decided to stay at home in the fifth century A.D. rather than migrate to Britain. If you've ever studied German, you're bound to have been struck by the resemblance of many short, everyday German words to their English counterparts, e.g., *wer ist das?* "who is that?," *trink Wasser!* "drink water!," *und* "and," *Hand* "hand," *Bett* "bed," *jung* "young," *gross* "large" (and the disparaging "gross" of American English), *Hund* "hound" (and compare this to Gothic *hunds*), *Garten* "garden." (Note, incidentally, that in German ordinary nouns have initial capital letters, not only proper nouns as is the case in English. This German habit may seem pretty wacky, but it was also the usual practice in English spelling during the eighteenth century.) Many people who don't speak German will assure you that it is a "harsh" language, but in truth it has a pleasantly melodious lilt to it, especially when spoken with a Rhineland accent.

The reason short German words often resemble short English ones stems from the fact that, as we've seen, Old High German was an extremely close relative of the language brought to Britain by the Anglo-Saxons. Basically, most short English words are part of our Anglo-Saxon heritage. But longer English words are different: They don't seem like German ones anymore. To take just three examples: The word "avoid" in German is *vermeiden,* while "commence" in German is *anfangen,* and "beautiful," *schön.*

The reason these longer English words don't seem like German ones is that they aren't part of the Anglo-Saxon heritage of English at all, but instead part of another heritage English enjoys, though at first this other heritage didn't *seem* very enjoyable.

And it's because English is the only modern Germanic language with this other heritage that it seems really quite different from any other modern Germanic tongue. We'll need to tell the story of that other heritage and the enormous impact it had on English. For the moment, let's look more closely at spelling in Anglo-Saxon times.

Chapter 6

How Anglo-Saxon
Spelling Evolved

He's an Anglo-Saxon Messenger—and those are
Anglo-Saxon attitudes.

—Lewis Carroll,
Through the Looking-Glass (1871)

MOST Anglo-Saxons couldn't read or write, and those who could were proud of their magical ability to do so. Tracing the evolution of the spelling of English during Anglo-Saxon times sounds as if it would be too remote from our own world, but in fact it's surprisingly interesting. Why? Because literate Anglo-Saxons were fascinated by the niceties of spelling and could even be fairly obsessive about it. I can't imagine Clair-Marie (or Lynne Truss, for that matter) being very happy in Anglo-Saxon Britain, but at least their love of accuracy would have been to a certain extent placated.

We've seen how the English language was born when the first Germanic invaders set foot in the British Isles, sometime in the second half of the fifth century A.D. The Saxons were accompanied by other Germanic tribes: the Angles and the Jutes, though these appear to have been less numerous than the Saxons themselves. Still, the Angles must have been an influential element in the three tribes, for they gave their name not only to England but also to its new language, English.

The term "Anglo-Saxon," used to describe the Germanic invaders, is actually a comparatively modern term; it was first used in the early seventeenth century to mean an English Saxon as opposed to a Continental one. The use of the same term to describe the Old English language is an even more recent innovation; it only dates from the late eighteenth century.

While the story of the English *language* begins with the invasion of Britain by Germanic tribes, the story of English *spelling* only really starts with the conversion of the Anglo-Saxons to Christianity in A.D. 597. This, as we've seen, was to lead to the eventual adoption by the Anglo-Saxons of the Roman alphabet, and to a modified and enhanced form of it which they employed as their own alphabet. In fact, Christianity in Britain had not one but two roots, a Roman and an Irish one. Irish monks were settling in Northumbria at around the same time as Saint Augustine went to Britain. Roman and Irish missionaries continued this work, and soon the Anglo-Saxons were a Christian people.

Runic writing in Anglo-Saxon persisted until the conversion; after that it was soon discarded because of its pagan connotations. Still, it had very likely worked well enough, and just because there are so few surviving examples of Anglo-Saxon writing shouldn't lead us to think that runic writing wasn't important. After all, the love letters we wrote (and sometimes received) as teenagers don't usually survive, but they were important at the time.

Those Old English manuscripts that survive from this early period of the English conversion show the importance of Irish teaching, for the script used was based on the Irish version of the Roman alphabet. At this point we are of course still close to 1,000 years before the invention of printing. The only way for written material to be produced was by hand.

As far as is known, the first formal documents written in the new Anglo-Saxon alphabet were law codes dating from the seventh century (but available today only in twelfth-century copies). The great Anglo-Saxon scholar the Venerable Bede, who was born in 672 or 673 and lived until 735, is known to have made translations from Latin into his daily language, Anglo-Saxon, but these translations have not survived. Doubtless much other Anglo-Saxon scholastic work failed to last to be enjoyed by posterity, or at least by those who could read it.

By the ninth century, the rate of production of written Anglo-Saxon seems to have increased; in any event, there are fairly numerous legal documents that survive from this period, though again they are only available in manuscripts written in later centuries. There are also more comprehensive glosses, in Anglo-Saxon, of original Latin texts. But it is only from the time of Alfred the Great—who lived from 849 to 899 and was king of the Saxon kingdom of Wessex from 871 until his death—that records of written English start to be comprehensive enough for us to trace the history of English spelling in some detail.

Alfred, for most people the best-known (indeed, often the only known) early English king, was not in fact king of England but king of the western region then known as Wessex, and also known as this again today for certain administrative purposes.

While in global terms Britain is only a small island, it was big enough, in the days of the Anglo-Saxons, to be conveniently divided into regional kingdoms. Most people never went farther than a day's walk from their hometown or village during their entire lives; it is hardly surprising that everyone took for granted that there would be kings of different parts of Britain. A Kentish serf was about as likely to see Wessex, let alone Mercia in the middle of Britain or Northumbria in the north, as he was to see Rome.

And so in the centuries after the Anglo-Saxons came to Britain, numerous small kingdoms appeared in what is now just one country, England. Gradually the stronger kingdoms absorbed the weaker ones—rather as competing corporations of today take over less successful players in the market—until by the end of the eighth century there were only three dominant players left.

These were Northumbria, which extended from the estuary of the river Humber up to the Firth of Forth in what is modern Scotland; Mercia, the kingdom of the Midlands; and Wessex, the area ruled by the West Saxons. Wessex covered England south of the Thames and by the ninth century also included Kent.

During the ninth century, Danish Vikings attacking from the east managed to subjugate Northumbria and Mercia, which in effect became Viking possessions. Still, once the Vikings had won control of these territories they ruled them in a relatively civilized and benevolent fashion. Not even the Vikings wanted to loot and pillage all the time, and besides, once they had conquered a region, any further looting and pillaging would only be something they were doing to themselves. One of many reasons for Alfred's greatness was that he fought a successful rearguard action in Wessex that confined the Vikings to the north and east of a line extending roughly from London to Derby.

It's easy to see where in Britain the Vikings made an impact. The Viking word for a village was *by* (this word is still used in modern English in a word such as "bylaw," which means a village law or a local law). In many parts of the Midlands and in the east of England, modern village names end with the suffix "by." I lived in the Midlands village of Wigston Magna, Leicestershire, for much of my teens. My brother and I went fishing near a village called Kilby. Two of Wigston's neighboring villages are Blaby and Arnesby (once the village of a Viking called *Arne*, which is still a popular Scandinavian male name today). As for Wigston, the name was once "Vikings Tun," or "town of the Vikings." Leicestershire is particularly rich in villages whose names make the Viking occupation seem like something that happened just last week.

Alfred's successors in the tenth century mustered their reserves of power and energy and went north to conquer the Danish areas, establishing the boundaries of England approximately where they stand today. And so, by the tenth century, England was unified under the West Saxon royal house.

Before this unification there were basically four regional dialects of Anglo-Saxon: the Northumbrian, Mercian, Kentish, and West Saxon dialects. Each dialect differed substantially in terms of pronunciation, spelling, and even grammar and vocabulary. It's difficult to gain an assessment of how readily comprehensible the different dialects were. Most likely they were not immediately mutually comprehensible, though they probably could be mastered quite quickly by someone from one region who went to live in another. The level of mutual incomprehensibility was probably not as strong as, say, the differences between modern Italian, French, and Spanish. All the same, the regional dialects of Anglo-Saxon had significant differences. Because of this, until the tenth century we should really think of Anglo-Saxon as a language consisting of the four dialects rather than a language that had established itself throughout the whole country. By the tenth century, with the West Saxons uniting England, the West Saxon way of spelling had become established as the standard used by King Alfred and his scribes, and as a standard that could be readily communicated around the entire country.

In effect this scribal tradition had succeeded in stabilizing the spelling of Anglo-Saxon and creating a single convention. Such a convention had never existed before, and there must have been many people who found that during their lives they were spelling English one way at the age of twenty and spelling it another way twenty or thirty years later, assuming they had managed to survive to such an age as fifty in Anglo-Saxon Britain, which was no trivial achievement in a time when nutrition was poor, diseases largely unchecked, and central heating absent.

There was something approximating a Golden Age of Anglo-Saxon in the second half of the tenth century. Under the reign of King Edgar, who ruled from A.D. 959 to 975, England was at last united and free from external attack. Another event helped contribute to a stable climate for spelling: a reform of the Benedictine order that revitalized monastic life throughout Britain. After a period when monasteries had experienced a decline in their populations, there were suddenly many new people taking up Holy Orders, which naturally led to a sudden heavy demand for books both in Latin and in the vernacular.

There is much splendid poetry in Anglo-Saxon; the language seems curiously well suited to poems about isolation, hardship, and a sense of being cut off from one's native tribes and origins. Perhaps the Anglo-Saxons often felt a homesickness for their German homeland. If you were a literate Anglo-Saxon living in around A.D. 975, these might have been the first few lines of one of your favorite poems:

> *Mæg ic be me sylfum soðgied wrecan*
> *siþas secgan hu ic geswincdagum*
> *earfoðwile oft þrowade*
> *bitre breostceare gebidan hæbbe*
> *gecunnad in ceole cearselda fela*
> *atol yþa gewealc*

which can be freely translated as

> *I may tell a true tale about myself,*
> *reveal a mariner's life,*
> *How I suffered days of unending toil,*
> *endured cares and bitter strife within my breast,*
> *my ship's keel cleaving*
> *endless vaults of heaving waves.*

These are the first lines of a rather wonderful Anglo-Saxon poem christened "The Seafarer" by scholars. The entire poem gives a vivid, truly chilly sense of the austere, cold, wet, elemental life of an Anglo-Saxon sailor; a life which, for all its privations and miseries, must have had potential for a kind of chilly heroism. The poem is found in just one manuscript, inscribed in about A.D. 975 and untitled. It might, of course, have been composed at some earlier time and entered in the manuscript by a scribe copying it from elsewhere; equally, the scribe might have been its author—we don't know the name of the poet, nor indeed whether he (or she) was a sailor.

By the year A.D. 1000—a year the Anglo-Saxons understandably regarded as poignantly significant for their culture and for their destiny as fervent Christians—the West Saxon scribal tradition was heading toward what was, in retrospect, to be its peak. Even the fact that so many documents were often written in English was remarkable in a Europe where the vernacular (which in France, for instance, would have been the Old French that had evolved from Vulgar Latin) was often regarded as merely a language to speak and not something to be accorded the exalted status of being *written down*. But even back in the tenth century the English were proud of their own language and produced many written documents in it.

We've seen how Alfred the Great himself encouraged this process by instigating a series of translations from Latin for the benefit of a people whom he considered to be intellectually impoverished by their own laziness and by the stress of Viking invasions. The stabilization of spelling was helped by the fact that English became widely used in the production of books at around the same time when large numbers of books were being produced. As Donald Scragg explains in his insightful work *A History of English Spelling*:

> By the end of the tenth century, the speed at which books had to be copied, the new and firm control exercised over the monastic orders who were the main producers of books, the fact that most if not all surviving writings are the products of professional scribes, and the new political unity of England all helped to create a single, stable orthography for English. These developments had a profound effect on the history of spelling.

In many respects, the English language during the first half of the eleventh century A.D. was in a similar situation to modern English today. Whatever we may think of the apparent irregularities and illogicalities of the spelling of the modern English language, there is at least a consistent standard for spelling almost every word.

This standard is enshrined in modern dictionaries, but its existence depends more upon what is in effect a *consensus* among those who read and write the English language. There are certainly excellent pieces of writing done in regional dialects—Irvine Welsh's *Trainspotting*, for example—but as I pointed out when I discussed that book earlier, there is no standard way of spelling the Edinburgh dialect and so Irvine Welsh had to invent his own way. It was much the same for the readers and writers of Anglo-Saxon during the first half of the eleventh century. All writing throughout England comformed to the same West Saxon standard, and many books survive from this period. There was some variation in regional spelling, but on the whole the standard prevailed.

So what was the spelling of Anglo-Saxon like during this period, the last half-century before the tumultuous events of 1066 that changed England—and English—forever?

The Roman alphabet used in the West Saxon spelling tradition was substantially the same as the one we use today for modern English. The letters *Q* and *Z* did exist nominally in the Anglo-Saxon alphabet, but the Anglo-Saxons usually tried to avoid them. For example, the modern English words "queen" and "quick" were perfectly familiar to the Anglo-Saxons but were spelled as *cwen* and *cwic*, respectively. (Incidentally, the vowel in *cwen* would have been a short vowel in Anglo-Saxon, like the vowel sound in the word "bed.") The Anglo-Saxons did sometimes use a *Q* or *Z* in foreign names, such as in the name "Elizabeth," destined to be so important in English history and which came into fashion in Anglo-Saxon times. There was also, for example, the Anglo-Saxon word *reliquias* ("relics"), which was a learned borrowing from Latin. *Q* and *Z* were much more widespread in French, and the flood of French and Romance loanwords that accompanied the French invasion after 1066 made English writers familiar with them, but *Z* has always had to fight *S* for its existence in English and even today, particularly in

British spellings, remains one of the least used members of our alphabet.

The only other really significant difference between the Anglo-Saxon alphabet and the modern English one was that, as we've seen, the Anglo-Saxons used four additional letters: ash, eth, thorn, and soon-superceded wyn.

Let's take a look now at the West Saxon spelling system in action. A useful way of illustrating the changing nature of spelling in the late Anglo-Saxon and early Middle English period is by showing the different ways in which the first few lines of the Lord's Prayer were written. This approach makes sense because it is a text that is readily available in a variety of types of Anglo-Saxon and early Middle English.

The accomplished prose writer Abbot Ælfric was trained at Winchester in the heart of the West Saxon kingdom and was known even in his own time for being a particularly good writer, which in those days meant not only that you knew how to use words but also that your writing had a beautiful physical appearance. Here is how he wrote the first few lines of the Lord's Prayer in his West Saxon of A.D. 990. This is, if you like, writing from the classical heyday of the West Saxon scribal tradition.

þu ure fæder, þe eart on heofonum, sy þin nama gehal-god. Cume ðin rice. Sy ðin wylla on eorðan swaswa on heofonum. Syle us todæg urne dæghwamlican hlaf. And forgyf us ure gyltas swaswa we forgyfað ðamþe wið us agyltað. And ne læd ðu na us on costnunge, ac alys us fram yfele.

The West Saxon standard did not quite achieve its zenith until the eleventh century. To get an idea of how different spelling could be in another region of England earlier in the tenth century, compare these lines written by Ælfric with a passage written in Northumbria about twenty years earlier, in around A.D. 970. It's a gloss of an illuminated seventh-century Latin manuscript known as the Lindisfarne Gospels:

Fader urer ðu arð in heofnum, sie gehalgud noma ðin. Tocymeð ric ðin. Sie willo ðin suæ is in heofne ond in eorðo. Hlaf userne ofer wistlic sel us todæg. Ond forgef us scylda usra suæ uoe forgefon scyldgum usum. Ond ne inlæd usih in costunge, ah gefrig usich from yfle.

Clearly, this passage is rather different from Ælfric's. It shows that there were still some variant regional spellings in use in the tenth century.

By around A.D. 1050, though, those regional variations had mostly disappeared. The West Saxon spelling convention ruled the roost and English was now only being spelled in one way. It's also interesting to note that the West Saxon spelling standard actually had a pretty consistent linkage between the sounds of the language and the way the sounds were spelled—a much more consistent linkage, in fact, than is found in modern English spelling.

Had the Anglo-Saxons been left to run England in peace, very likely the West Saxon spelling convention, with its Germanic background, would have become even more dominant during the second half of the eleventh century. The West Saxon convention would, in fact, probably have developed into a modern spelling convention. As for the English language today, it would have most likely evolved into something approximately midway between the modern Dutch and German languages: That is, it would contain elements of the "High German" of modern German and the "Low German" of modern Dutch, for both these influences are detectable in the Germanic element of modern English.

Of course, we can't know for certain what English today would be like if it had remained purely a Germanic language, and, in any case, studying the story of language and writing is difficult enough without worrying too much about hypothetical situations. For as things turned out, it was the destiny of English *not* to remain a purely Germanic language. The great change that now came over the English language and the English cultural heritage had a massive and far-reaching effect on the very fibers of the spoken English language. And, because a written language is always a reflection of a spoken language, the huge changes that came over spoken English were naturally mirrored in how English was written. Indeed, the great changes still resonate through spoken and written English even today.

The trigger for these changes was the arrival in England

in 1066 of William I of Normandy—known by history as William the Conqueror—who reached the southern English coast with a few thousand able and skilled soldiers in tow, and a determination to become master of the British Isles.

Chapter 7

The Norman Conquest

The Norman Conquest was a Good Thing, as from this time onwards England stopped being conquered and thus was able to become top nation.

—W. C. Sellar and R. J. Yeatman,
1066 and All That (1930)

HE invasion of Celtic Britain and of the last vestiges of Roman Britain by the Angles, the Saxons, and the Jutes is the most important factor behind the creation of the English language. Then, on Monday, September 27, 1066, during a bout of particularly cold and rainy weather, William the First of Normandy—his ancestors were Vikings who had settled in northern France—embarked with an army for the southeast coast of England. William's invasion is the second most important reason why the English language is the way it is.

It's not known for certain how many men William had with him, but factoring in logistical and communications considerations, he was most likely accompanied by no more than about 7,000 cavalry and infantry, and quite possibly as few as 5,000. That is, he had with him about the same number of spectators you might find today attending a minor league sporting event. Not much of an army, really, when you consider the splendor of the prize he was trying to win.

William landed the following morning. During the next fortnight he took the unresisting towns of Pevensey and Hastings, then began to march north. On October 13, about five miles north of Hastings (the town there is known today, appropriately enough, as Battle), William encountered the army of Harold, the Anglo-Saxon king.

The Anglo-Saxons were worn out. They had just marched more than 200 miles from the north, where they had defeated the invading forces of Harald Hardraade, king of Norway, and killed Hardraade himself. Most likely because of the exhausted state of his army, Harold decided to take up an initially defensive position against William. Had William given the Anglo-Saxons a few days to recuperate, the subsequent history of Britain might have been very different. But, perhaps aware—or having guessed—how exhausted the defenders were, William would not tolerate any delay. The following morning, Friday, October 14, he launched an attack against the Anglo-Saxon forces.

First, the Normans began attacking with archers and cavalry. The Norman archers were feared for their lethality. But the Anglo-Saxons were fighting for their lives— and their country. They managed to beat the Normans back, and almost drove them from the field. Yet William's leadership, and no doubt the promises he had made to his men of rich pickings, rallied his forces. Eventually, the Normans' confidence and comparative freshness won the day. Harold's brothers were killed early in the battle. Toward nightfall on October 14 Harold was himself killed—according to legend by an arrow that struck him in the eye.

After his great victory, William proceeded to move against possible centers of resistance in England so quickly that he prevented a new English leader from emerging. The poor communications of the time helps to explain how it was possible for William to take over Britain—which had at the time a population of about one million—with such a small army. He also undoubtedly won local support for his side, mainly because he was quite happy to leave the ordinary Anglo-Saxons to continue living in the way they had before, so long as they accepted him and his cronies as their new masters. He was a conqueror, not an oppressor.

Besides, William thought right was on his side, for he believed he had a legitimate claim to the English throne. According to Norman French historians (admittedly, hardly an unbiased bunch), Harold himself—when he'd been Earl of Wessex—had promised William the English throne on the demise of King Edward the Confessor, who had died childless on January 5, 1066. Not surprisingly, William did his utmost to spread details of his legitimate claim around the country that was his new acquisition.

Very likely, most Anglo-Saxon peasants, who knew far

more about cabbages than kings, let alone anything about the niceties of succession law, were as ready to believe William's version of the story as anybody else's, especially when the prize for believing William was the privilege of not receiving an arrow from a Norman bow. William was also helped in his successful campaign by his own previous experience as a ruler, and by the strength of his personality. He was known to be a hard but fair man, and he quickly won respect even from the people he had defeated.

William was crowned king of England on Christmas Day 1066 in Westminster Abbey, a day that can be usefully taken to mark the formal conclusion of the Norman conquest in England. Unrest and rebellions continued sporadically in some parts of England, but within five years of the Norman invasion, all resistance was quashed. England was now a Norman country.

The most immediate political change that came over England following the Norman Conquest was the destruction of the native Anglo-Saxon aristocracy, all of whose lands were given to Normans and many of whom were killed. For the ordinary Anglo-Saxons, though, life continued much as it had before except that now their rulers on both a national and local level were Norman French aristocrats. These new rulers initially spoke no Anglo-Saxon apart from, doubtless, a few harsh words they used when they wanted to tell their servants what to do for them. This dynamic of ruler and ruled paved the way for a massive linguistic change in England.

In the first few decades following the Norman Conquest, many Norman French people migrated to England to swell the ranks of those who had come to the country with William or who had subsequently been appointed to high positions by him. A strange situation developed where for about 200 years England had two living languages: Norman French and Anglo-Saxon. Norman French became the language of the ruling class and remained important as the court language and the medium of parliament and the law until as late as the fourteenth century.

The formerly unique position of English (i.e., Anglo-Saxon) as the only vernacular of Europe that was extensively used in official documents and had a fully developed, standardized literary form was lost. This wasn't because the Norman conquerors held the English language in any sort of inherent contempt (though doubtless some did), but rather because the number of Norman French immigrants was sufficient for their own language to be established and maintained as the language of everyday social life, business, and law.

And of course, Norman French was voluntarily mastered by many native English speakers because of the social prestige they hoped to gain by doing so. The different social strata of the new Norman French aristocracy and the English peasants who waited on them in every sense were established during this period, conferring a high status upon the Norman French language and relegating the native Anglo-Saxon tongue to inferior status.

A linguistically revealing example of the different social status of Norman French and Anglo-Saxon people during the period after the Norman Conquest is shown in how often—or how rarely—the Anglo-Saxons got to eat meat.

We might assume that the ordinary Anglo-Saxons would rarely have tasted flesh at all unless it derived from a night's poaching or from an unlucky rabbit. This assumption can be proven linguistically. After the Norman Conquest, Anglo-Saxons referred to farm animals by their own Anglo-Saxon words, such as *swin, scep*—the *sc* in this word was pronounced as *sh*—and *ku*. These Anglo-Saxon words give us, today, the modern words "swine," "sheep," and "cow."

The counterpart of these words in Norman French were *porc, mouton,* and *boeuf* (for clarity I am using the modern French spellings of these words). Initially, the Norman French words—like the Anglo-Saxon ones— also simply referred to the *animals*: the pig, the sheep, and the cow. But in the new, hybrid English language that slowly began to come into being—basically Anglo-Saxon but with more and more Norman French words infiltrating it—the original Norman French words gained a meaning that referred to the animal *after it had arrived on a plate set down in front of a wealthy Norman French lord or landowner*. The brutal fact that the Norman French ate better than the Anglo-Saxons who waited on them is now captured forever in this derivation of the English names for these meats: "pork," "mutton," and "beef." We don't, for example, eat "pig," and by all accounts neither did many Anglo-Saxons.

Throughout the two centuries following the Norman French invasion, the rivalry between the two cultures and social classes continued, though as time went on it became somewhat more harmonious. The class system in England has its origins in the Norman Conquest. In a sense the rivalry between the ruling class and the subordinate class persists today and would doubtless be much worse had not economic prosperity improved living conditions for the modern counterparts of the Anglo-Saxon class, and had not the development of a more technological society put a premium on talent, merit, and hard work, enabling even the lowly born to acquire wealth and status.

There are still echoes of the Norman French/Anglo-Saxon rivalry in popular culture. In many novels and films—including many Hollywood ones—villains are inadvertently or deliberately given "villainous" Norman French names and the heroes "good, honest" Anglo-Saxon names. For instance, in J. K. Rowling's Harry Potter stories, the character Harry Potter (an Anglo-Saxon name if ever there was one) struggles against Draco Malfoy (Malfoy was actually a popular Norman French surname). Significantly, Malfoy is portrayed as being from a wealthier and more socially elevated background than Harry and his friends. Similarly, in James Cameron's movie *Titanic* (1997), the impoverished hero Jack Dawson (another eminently Anglo-Saxon name) is contrasted with the Norman French–sounding name of his wealthy, dishonest (if resourceful) rival in love: Caledon Hockley.

Yet despite the natives' lower status in the period following the Norman Conquest, the Anglo-Saxon language didn't die out completely. Far from doing so, the Anglo-Saxon language continued as the basis of English; what was interesting was what happened to it.

Why didn't Anglo-Saxon die out? Well, for one thing, there were far more Anglo-Saxons than Normans in Britain. Many Norman French speakers found it convenient to learn some Anglo-Saxon in order to give orders to their underlings. At the same time, more and more Norman French words were adopted by socially ambitious Anglo-Saxons into their native Anglo-Saxon. In addition, a good deal of intermarrying took place between the Normans and Anglo-Saxons—at a practical level because there were simply not enough Norman French women (or men, for that matter) to go around.

What about written English? Because English ceased for those two centuries to be the most prestigious language in England, there was a great reduction in the output of written material in English. Throughout the entire Anglo-Saxon period, written English had always been the prerogative of scribes, priests, and other educated people, all of whom were in a great minority, probably constituting no more than two or three percent of the population.

In fact, during the period after the Norman Conquest, Anglo-Saxon was abandoned as a language for writing official documents such as government decrees and legal statutes. The reason for this was that the people for whom such material was intended—the new governors and local potentates—could at first neither speak English nor read it, and didn't have much desire to do so. Not that many of them could read Norman French, either. Ironically, literacy among the new Norman aristocracy was even less widespread than it was in late Anglo-Saxon England.

So we mustn't necessarily think of the Normans as a refined, highly educated, and literate Continental elite. Of course, it was in the interests of the Normans to put it about that the Anglo-Saxons were primitive peasants, but closer to the truth was that the Anglo-Saxon culture had been a strong and dignified one. The Norman French culture did not add much to it but rather replaced it with something that was in many respects less good, and certainly much less *English*.

Because comparatively little written English survives from the period from about 1100 to 1300, it's difficult to chronicle the development of the English language (and English spelling) during that period. The closest we can get to knowing what went on appears to be that at first the West Saxon literary tradition and spelling standard was maintained, but it gradually declined with the inexperience and lack of training of those scribes who did write in English during the next two centuries.

The result was that by about 1300 many variations were

arising in how English was pronounced and spelled. Let's look at a passage of English in the middle of this transitional period when English spelling had no established standard. Here are the first few lines of the Lord's Prayer, written in the Anglo-Saxon of 1200:

Fader ure, þu þe ert on heofene, sye þin name gehalged. Tobecume þin rice. Gewurde þin gewille on eorðan swaswa on heofenan. Ure dayghwamlice hlaf syle us to-dayg. And forgyf us ure geltas swaswa we forgyfeð ure geltenden. *And* ne læd þu us on costnunge, ac ales us of yfele.

In this passage there is a noticeable reduction of many classical Anglo-Saxon inflectional endings (such as *-um, -a, -ne,* and *-an*) to a uniform *-e,* which denoted the vowel sound represented today by the *a* in the word "about." The simplification of Anglo-Saxon had started, and the Anglo-Saxon spoken two centuries earlier had in a very real sense already been superseded.

The reason for the reductions in the inflections at the end of the Anglo-Saxon words is that the contact between Anglo-Saxon and Norman French was actually tending to simplify to some extent the grammar of *both* languages. When two groups of people speaking different languages mingle socially and at work, there is always a pressure toward grammatical simplification in order to aid the process of communication. This is exactly what happened here.

The passage quoted above was written in Canterbury. This cathedral city was an important location for the continuity of Anglo-Saxon during the Middle Ages because of the enduring importance of Canterbury as the seat of the mother church of England. In fact, the Anglo-Saxon that was written at Canterbury became a kind of regional semistandard for English during the period when Norman French still dominated as the language of the ruling class.

As for the language itself, it continued to develop into a grammatically more simplified version of the original Anglo-Saxon. By 1340 Canterbury scribes were writing the same first lines of the Lord's Prayer like this:

Vader oure, þet art ine heuenes, yhalged by þi-name. Cominde þi riche. Yworþe þi wil ase ine heuene and ine erþe. Bread oure echedayes yef ous today. And uorlet ous oure yeldinges ase and we norleteþ oure yelderes. And ne ous led nagt into uondinge, ac vri ous uram queade.

In this new version, the letter eth has disappeared and the letter thorn is being used both for the voiced and unvoiced *th*-sound. Also, some new vocabulary is being employed: For example, another Germanic word, "bread" in its modern form (and spelling), has replaced the Anglo-Saxon word "hlaf," which survives today only in the surname "Lafford," an originally Anglo-Saxon surname that meant, literally, "bread-lord"; an owner or master, or even simply a baker of bread.

The Anglo-Saxon language continued to change profoundly under the influence of a desire for simplification of grammatical structure to reduce confusion among bilingual speakers. Another crucial factor was the borrowing of more and more Norman French words into Anglo-Saxon, so that by the late fourteenth century, English was starting to look much more like modern English than Anglo-Saxon ever did.

The following famous passage was written in about the year 1390. Notice how different it is from the passage quoted above that was written in Canterbury in 1340. The reason is that the writer of the Canterbury passage would have been a cleric deeply versed in the Anglo-Saxon tradition. However, the writer of the following passage was a poet named Geoffrey Chaucer (1342/43–1400), who was very much a man of the world and worked as a diplomat and political fixer among the Norman French. The English he wrote was rather consciously loaded with Norman French words and ways of thinking. He was also a genius, and, while not a religious cleric, certainly wrote like an angel.

Furthermore, Chaucer's own dialect, the East Midlands dialect of English, was the one destined to become the standard for the entire country, whereas the Canterbury passage quoted above is written in the Kentish dialect that was eventually relegated to a mere provincial style and subsequently abandoned.

Notice, generally, how modern Chaucer's writing seems. By the time he was writing, the English language had changed into something new, which scholars conveniently refer to as Middle English. There is no definite point, no particular year, at which Middle English took over from Anglo-Saxon, especially as there are early and late forms of Middle English as well as many regional variations. However, it is very clear that the passage below is a different language from, say, the Anglo-Saxon of King Alfred and the 1340 Canterbury passage. One certainly cannot imagine that Chaucer and Alfred would have found each other's language mutually comprehensible. English had changed, and there was no turning back.

Here is Chaucer at work:

> *Whan that aprill with his shoures soote*
> *The droghte of march hath perced to the root,*
> *And bathed ever veyne in swich licour*
> *Of which vertu engendred is the flour;*
> *Whan zephirus eek with with his sweete breeth*
> *Inspired hath in every holt and heeth*
> *The tendre croppes, and the yonge sonne*
> *Hath in the ram his halve cours yronne . . .*
> *Than longen folk to goon on pilgrimages*
> *And palmeres for to seken straunge strondes*
> *To ferne halwes, kowthe in sondry londes*
> *And specialy from every shires ende*
> *Of Engelonde to Canterbury they wend,*
> *The holy blissful martyr for to seke*
> *That hem hath holpen what than they were seke.*

These are, with a small cut in the middle, the first lines of the General Prologue to Chaucer's *Canterbury Tales*. This is a rather contrived but unquestionably brilliant uncompleted long poem that tells the story of a pilgrimage made by a cross-section of medieval society from Southwark in London to Canterbury. The poem recounts the tales the pilgrims rather implausibly tell along the way in order to entertain one another. I must admit I've never quite understood how anyone could have heard anything above the sound of the horses' hooves and the carriage wheels, but that's poetic license for you. The pilgrims never actually *reach* Canterbury—ironically in view of the title of the work—as Chaucer evidently lost interest in the project some way down the line and abandoned it. I have always agreed with H. G. Wells, who thought he would have preferred the pilgrims to have done more living along the way and told fewer tales. Still, some of the tales themselves are great masterpieces, and interesting for a much wider range of reasons than for their linguistic appeal. If ever you imagine that medieval literature must be boring and pious, check out "The Miller's Tale" from *The Canterbury Tales* and prepare to be surprised. In this tale it is almost regarded as a crime against nature to return to your *own* bed after using the outhouse in the middle of the night. Perhaps medieval life really was like this.

The language of the General Prologue looks to us much more like the modern English we know and love than anything we've seen so far in tracing the story of English writing. Still, the language is different from modern English, and sometimes seems extremely unfamiliar, as in the line *To ferne halwes, kowthe in sondry londes,* where three Anglo-Saxon words, *ferne, halwes,* and *kowthe,* which seem completely foreign to us, are being used. (They mean, respectively: distant, shrines, and known.) But on the whole it is the unfamiliar *spelling* of this passage that makes it appear rather more incomprehensible than it needs to be. If Chaucer is read aloud by someone who can pronounce the words as it is believed they were pronounced in his day, the language does not sound quite as alien as it looks in this passage.

Translating Chaucer is fun, so I have had a go at translating these lines, keeping the translation close to the original so that direct comparison of the words is possible.

> *When that April with his showers sweet*
> *The drought of March has pierced to the root*
> *And bathed every vein in such liquor*
> *That is the flower of created life* [vertu *meant something*
>   *like a "life force" or "life energy"*],
> *When Zephirus* [*the west wind personified as a god*] *also*
>   *with his sweet breath*
> *Has inspired in every copse and heath*
> *Tender crops, and the young sun*
> *Has in the Ram* [*an old name for the constellation Aries*]
>   *run half his course . . .*
> *Then people long to go on pilgrimages*
> *And pilgrims go to seek strange shores,*
> *To distant shrines, well known in various lands.*

And especially from every county's end
Of England to Canterbury they wend
The holy blessed martyr [i.e., Saint Thomas à Becket] for to
  seek
Who helped them out when they were sick.

Chaucer was a great writer, and his use of English is strong, uncompromising, and in its own way quite modern. We need to remember, however, that when Chaucer was writing there were still many regional variations of Middle English. There was not a consistent spelling standard, or anything like it, and most scribes very much did their own thing, using spellings they thought made sense. They were not even consistent to their *own* usages and let these vary from one day to the other. Consider the following two versions of the Lord's Prayer, both written in Middle English, though at different times. The first dates from 1375 and the second from 1450.

1375

Fader oure þat is in heuen,
Blessid be þi name to neuen.
Come to vs þi kyngdome.
In heuen and erthe þi wille be done.
Oure ilk-day-bred graunt vs today,
And oure mysdedes forgyue vs ay.
Als we do hom þat trespas us
Right so haue merci v on vs,

And lede vs in no foundynge,
Bot shild vs fro al wicked þinge.

1450

Owre fadur þat art in hewon,
Blessed be þi name to newon.
Cum to vs þi kyndome.
In hewon and erthe þi wyl be done.
Owre ilke days bred grawnt vs today,
And owre mysdedus forgyf vs ay.
As we do hom þat to vs trespas
Ryght so haue mercy vpon vs,
And lede vs into no fowndyng,
But schyld vs fro all wyccud þing.

It's easy to see that there are many spelling differences between these two passages, as well as differences in how the
language is used grammatically—although the last line of
each passage, for example, is simply: "But shield us from
every wicked thing." Clearly, the language was not only in
a state of flux but also its spelling had really ceased to have
any effective standard whatsoever.

Both the scribes alternate between the letter *i* and *y* in
positions where the vowel is stressed; both display a willingness to use the final *-e* in a fairly random way; and
sometimes a double consonant will be used at the end of a
word where the other writer prefers a single consonant.
No one could look at these two passages and think there

was any consistent spelling standard in use. Rather, it appears to be a language whose writers imagine they can spell pretty much as they wish.

It's quite difficult for us to imagine the situation the spelling of Middle English was in at this point in its history. No matter how illogical the spelling of modern English may seem, the standard is absolutely dominant and there are in fact few words that can be spelled legitimately in more than one way (one example is the word "jail," which can also be spelled as "gaol," but the second spelling seems to be on the way out). The lack of a national standard for Middle English was complicated by the fact that different regions tended to prefer different ways of spelling. These often—though not always—reflected regional differences in pronunciation. There are even examples of pieces of writing from the Middle English period where the same scribe spells a word differently in different places in the writing, sometimes in places quite close together.

Middle English is essentially a hybrid version of Norman French and Anglo-Saxon. While it is certainly more accurate to speak of it as Anglo-Saxon profoundly affected by Norman French rather than vice versa, the French influence is so great that there are occasions where it really is not entirely clear which language is most influencing the other. The heritage of modern English as a language composed of Germanic and Romance elements is an important reason why English is so intriguing and expressive a tongue.

We have already seen that there will be a tendency for simplification of both languages where people speaking two different languages are brought into regular, day-to-day contact. Middle English itself can be described not only as a hybrid, but also as a *convenient simplification* that contains elements of both the languages from which it derives. To quantify this, it is useful to point out that the modern English we speak every day consists of about sixty percent of words that derive from Anglo-Saxon, with the remaining forty percent deriving from Norman French, French, or Latin and sometimes from more than one. These percentages are not exact—we have already seen that many English words come from other foreign languages—but they are a useful guide to how the substance of modern English has been formed. By about 1450, this ratio of sixty percent Anglo-Saxon to forty percent Norman French/French/Latin was already well on its way to being established.

The continuing process of hybridization led to continuing simplifications of the structure of Middle English. As a result, modern English (and, in fact, English from about the fifteenth century onward) is completely devoid of what we can describe as "unnecessary" grammatical factors: It makes very little use of variable noun endings and even has a comparatively simple system for verbs. The only real area of difficulty with verbs is that some common verbs deriving from Anglo-Saxon retain the "strong" form for the imperfect and past perfect (such as "sing," "sang," "has sung"). There used to be more strong verb forms (for example, in *The Canterbury Tales* passage quoted above Chaucer writes *holpen* for "helped"), but the remaining strong forms are still very important today.

Modern English also has no grammatical gender for nouns whatsoever. English distinguishes between gender in the singular pronouns such as "he" and "she" and their other grammatical forms, but in the plural of the pronoun forms it does not even do this: "they" can mean men and women, or only men or only women. Most European languages of Indo-European descent have masculine and feminine noun genders—and a neuter as well, in some languages such as German and Russian. Noun gender can seem illogical (for example, the German word for "girl" is actually a neuter word, *das Mädchen,* because diminutives in German take neuter endings), and gender varies from one language to another: For example, the word for "table" is feminine in French (*la table*) but masculine in German (*der Tisch*). Noun gender simply has to be painstakingly mastered when you learn these languages. Without grammatical gender, all the problems of singular and plural adjectival "agreement" with nouns—arguably an entirely pointless grammatical device—vanish.

Another outcome of the hybridization of the original Anglo-Saxon after the French invasion is that, like Middle English, modern English often has both a Germanic and a Romance word *for the same concept.* In almost all cases the Germanic use will tend to be more "down to earth" than the Romance one. (Think again of Harry Potter and Draco Malfoy.) This gives speakers and writers of English the chance to modulate what they are saying to adopt an appropriate tone. To take just one example: "Begin" (the Germanic word) means basically the same as "commence" (the Romance word), but the tone of the two words differs very greatly. Using "commence" in everyday speech would seem affected unless you wanted to achieve a deliberately pompous effect.

During the fifteenth century the borrowing of words from Norman French into English intensified. For example, the introduction of the Norman French word *trespas* can be seen in both versions of the Lord's Prayer cited above, from 1375 and 1450. It is a direct lifting of the old French word *trespas*, which meant "passing across" and came to mean a "transgression" or "sin" because of the idea of passing across from good to evil.

The Anglo-Saxon word *trespas* replaced was *gelt*, which was a version of the word *gylt* that meant a sin, a failure of duty, or an offense. One reason why modern English offers so many rich and expressive possibilities is that in many cases, even though French replacements for Anglo-Saxon words became part of the living Middle English language, the original Anglo-Saxon word was retained. So, for example, we still have the word "guilt," which is simply a modern spelling of the original Anglo-Saxon word. We also still have the word "trespass," which nowadays is used to describe a particular type of guilt: that relating to walking on somebody else's land when you have no right or permission. I was once walking in Oxfordshire and saw a sign at the gate of a large country estate. The gate was next to a church. The sign read:

> Unlike the institution on your left, we will not forgive you your trespasses.

This shows rather amusingly that while the word "trespass" is indeed mainly used nowadays to refer to trespassing on land, we still understand the meaning of the term as indicating a religious sin or failure of duty, although this use is now obsolete in everyday spoken English.

Not every Anglo-Saxon word that was replaced by a French word survived the experience. Still, many of them did—usually where the Anglo-Saxon word better filled a niche in terms of meaning than its French replacement, as in the words "guilt" and "trespass" in modern English. All the same, many Anglo-Saxon words have vanished completely from the language, and this explains why a modern English speaker learning Anglo-Saxon has to learn a fair amount of unfamiliar vocabulary. And, incidentally, why longer German words rarely seem familiar to us.

By around the year 1400, English spelling was still very inconsistent. But the Middle English first spoken in the East Midlands was reaching London and was on the way to becoming a national standard for the new hybrid language. This happened because during the fifteenth century the increasing importance of London as an administrative and commercial center began to influence the way English was spelled.

At the same time, Norman French was starting to lose its grip on the nation. Norman French was still used, but it was more and more regarded as a foreign language that had to be consciously taught and learned. The descendants of the Norman French who had invaded Britain nearly four centuries ago had at last begun to think of themselves as English. By the middle of the fifteenth century, Middle English was firmly established as the dominant language of England. Norman French was no longer one of the main languages of England, but its influence had been enormous, profound, and permanent.

At the most obvious level, Norman French had a great effect upon the vocabulary of Middle English. When English borrowed French words it was not, as it is today, a language used to borrowings. We might have expected that English would have borrowed French words and forced them into its own sound patterns. But in fact this did not happen, because the borrowings took place during a time when England was basically a bilingual country, and educated native English people tended to adopt a pronunciation for the borrowings that was close to the French original. This factor had an enormous impact on the way the borrowings were spelled. The high status of French led educated native English people to be happy with writing the borrowings in a way similar to the way they were written in French. This phenomenon often happens in the history of spelling: A high-status language yields loanwords whose spelling and pronunciation are often retained much as they were originally. A recent example might be the Italian word *latte,* used to describe a kind of milky coffee, which has been adopted in its Italian pronunciation and spelling by English due to its high-status associations with the fashionable Continental café culture.

During the Middle English period, French borrowings were spelled much as they were in the original French. For example, the French word *gentil* which led to the English word "gentle" retained the spelling of the French original almost intact. The meaning of the word has changed from the days of Middle English, when "gentle" meant wellborn and specifically someone who was entitled to bear a coat of arms. This meaning survives in modern English in the words "gentleman" and "gentlefolk" and also in the phrase "of gentle birth," but otherwise "gentle" now mainly means "mild" or "free from aggression."

Similarly, the word "chance" was spelled *chaunce* in Middle English, while the words "dance," "danger," and "desperation" were spelled, respectively, *daunce, daunger,* and *desperaunce* in Middle English. The words dropped the *u* by about 1700. Some words borrowed from Norman French have remained identical to how they were spelled in the Middle English period, such as "haunt," "jaundice," and "vaunt." There is no particular reason why this happened; it just seems to be the way these spellings developed.

During the Middle Ages, most educated people in England—whether of Norman French or Anglo-Saxon origin—also had a knowledge of Latin, which was the language of religious ceremonies, intellectual discourse, and scholarly writing. It was also a convenient international language for educated people traveling abroad or for Continentals crossing the Channel. But it was Norman French (and to a lesser extent Parisian French) that furnished the majority of the Romance loanwords to Middle English. The extent of these loans from French was astonishing. The full text of Chaucer's General Prologue, 858 lines in all, contains almost 500 different French loans. The loanwords are, as we might expect, words that have to do with many of the subtleties and pleasures of life as well as anything to do with enforcement of authority and the winning of power over others, such as in the legal system. Borrowings from Norman French into Middle English include:

Administration: *authority, bailiff, constable, duke, government, parliament, peasant, prince, revenue, traitor, tyrant, warden*

Law: *accuse, adultery, advocate, convict, crime, evidence, felon, fine, heir, prison, punishment, trespass, verdict, warrant*

Religion: *abbey, anoint, cardinal, cathedral, confess, heresy, immortality, saint, salvation, temptation, theology*

Leisure and the arts: *art, beauty, color, dalliance, dance, fool, melody, minstrel, music, noun, painting, poet, recreation, story, tournament, volume*

Food and drink: *appetite, bacon, beef, biscuit, cream, dinner, feast, fry, gravy, herb, mustard, mutton, pork, sugar, supper, vinegar*

Fashion: *apparel, boots, brooch, cape, diamond, dress, fashion, frock, fur, pearl, petticoat, robe, veil, wardrobe*

Military: *ambush, archer, army, besiege, captain, navy, peace, retreat, sergeant, soldier, spy*

Science and learning: *anatomy, calendar, copy, gender, grammar, logic, medicine, physician, study, surgeon*

The home: *basin, blanket, bucket, ceiling, chandelier, chimney, curtain, cushion, pantry, parlor, porch, towel, tower, turret*

The spelling of many of these words has remained much the same as when the words were first borrowed by Middle English.

Until about 1400 there was, in fact, also ample word-borrowing from Latin into Middle English, especially of words relating to administration and law (such as alias, arbitrator, client, conspiracy, legal, legitimate); science and learning (abacus, comet, contradiction, et cetera, index, inferior, library, major, mechanical, scribe); religion (diocese, immortal, infinite, pulpit, scripture); and many general "idea words" (such as admit, contempt, depression, exclude, expedition, interest, interrupt, lucrative, popular, private, solitary, substitute). But after about 1400 we find that most borrowings from Romance tongues came through the medium of Norman French rather than Latin, and the spelling of the borrowings correspondingly tends to reflect the Norman French rather than the Latin spelling. This development was probably due to the gradually diminishing importance of Latin, though one must be careful what one says here because Latin remained an important cultural language (and an international language) for several centuries.

A particular problem introduced by the extensive French borrowings concerned words that began with the letter *H*. The *h*-sound occurred in classical Latin, but it disappeared even from Latin in the first few centuries A.D. As a result, French—derived as it was from Latin—had never had the *h*-sound in all the French words that originated from Latin—which was the vast majority of them. Yet the influence of classical Latin spelling during the first thousand years of the Christian era was so strong that French scribes were more than ready to use the letter *H* at the start of words even where the sound had never appeared in French speech at all.

Many of these words that were *written* with an initial *H* but had never been spoken with one were borrowed by Middle English. There are basically three groups of them. The first, rather small, group consists of words where the initial *H* has now been lost from the spelling. It includes the words "able," "ability," and "arbor"; "arbor," for example, derives ultimately from the Latin word *herbarium*.

In the second group, the English spelling preserves the *H* but the words are pronounced without it. These words, which give schoolchildren so much trouble even today, include "heir," "honor," "honest," and "hour."

The third group is perhaps the most interesting, because here the original word was written with an *H* though pronounced without it, but in modern English the *h*-sound has been reintroduced. This phenomenon is known as *spelling pronunciation* and occurs where the spelling of a word has an influence on the way the word is pronounced.

Spelling pronunciation mainly derives from the sixteenth and seventeenth centuries and appears to have taken place at a time when there was still considerable flux in the way English was spelled and pronounced. During this period people often seemed to feel they had a choice between including the *h*-sound in the word when they spoke it or leaving it out—for example, the words "habit," "harmonious," and "heritage" were often pronounced without the *h*-sound.

Dr. Samuel Johnson, in his great *Dictionary* of 1755 (of which more later), records that the words "herb," "humble," and "humor" were pronounced without the initial *h*-sound, and indeed references to such pronunciation are common throughout nineteenth-century literature. In modern English the *h*-sound for these and other words beginning with a written *H* has stabilized, and standard English expects the *h*-sound to be pronounced.

Ironically, pronouncing these words without the *h*-sound is regarded nowadays in some quarters as indicative of the speech of people from working-class backgrounds, yet until comparatively recently it was in fact also seen as an indication of an *upper-class* background. A red-faced, rotund British gentleman, well soused with port and wine, might have spoken of "'orses and 'ounds" as he enjoyed his roast pheasant, confident that his listeners regarded him as an excellent specimen of British aristocratic humanity—the sort of person who gives the impression of being ennobled when he reaches a certain weight.

The use of the *h*-sound at the start of words influenced by spelling pronunciation has indeed become standard in modern English. One interesting relic of a time when these words did not always have their initial *h*-sound survives in the fact that some people even today prefer to use "an" rather than "a" before some words that are most definitely pronounced with the *h*-sound. These words include "hotel" and "historically." In fact, when we use "an" before these words, there is often a temptation to drop the initial *h*-sound because we are so used to using "an" before words that start with a vowel. Another relic of the past confusion in whether the *h*-sound was pronounced or not, and whether it was written or not, occurs in one spelling of "ostler," which has a variant spelling "hostler" that is occasionally seen even to this day, and certainly is seen in the closely related words "hostel" and "hostelry."

Spelling pronunciation, a phenomenon we will meet again shortly, has actually helped to narrow the gap between the spelling and pronunciation of modern English, which without spelling pronunciation would be even more disconnected than it is today.

The influence of Norman French on Middle English was so wide ranging that listing every aspect of the influence is a task for specialists and would require several chapters in itself. The point is that the influence existed and continues to exist, and that along with the Germanic heritage of modern English we also have a Norman French heritage that is an integral part of our spoken language, our written language, and our culture. Every day, hundreds of millions of users of English around the world speak and write sentences that contain Germanic and Norman French words next to each other without reflecting how strange it is that they are speaking and writing a language which—in a very literal sense—had two mothers.

Chapter 8

A Century of
Revolutionary Change

The worshipful father and first founder and embellisher
of ornate eloquence in our English, I mean Master
Geoffrey Chaucer.

> —William Caxton, from the Epilogue
> to his edition (c. 1478) of Chaucer's
> translation of *The Consolacion of
> Philosophie* by Boethius

IDDLE English looks a lot more like modern
English than Anglo-Saxon does, but even
Middle English doesn't look *enormously* like
modern English.

The strange thing is that the transition from Middle
English to modern English took place over only a century,
from around 1400 to around 1500. An old lady who was
born, say, in 1395 and died in 1500 would literally have
been speaking a different language as a child from the one
she would have spoken in her old age. This is a difficult
idea for us to grasp as modern English speakers, because

we have little problem understanding written English that dates back three or even four centuries from the present day. But the truth is that the century of revolutionary change in English from 1400 to 1500 involved greater change than anything that has happened to the English language in the past three or even four centuries prior to our present-day vantage point.

Before we look at this century-long revolution that transformed Middle English into modern English, a brief question. When we tell the story of English spelling, how valid is it, really, to categorize English into Anglo-Saxon, Middle English, and modern English?

Obviously, if things can be measured they can better be assessed, and from this point of view it is convenient to refer to Anglo-Saxon as the form of English spoken up to about A.D. 1100, Middle English as the version of the language used from A.D. 1100 to A.D. 1500, and modern English thereafter.

But in practice languages do not turn so abruptly from one form into another. Anglo-Saxon did not suddenly become Middle English on January 1, 1100, any more than Middle English suddenly became modern English on January 1, 1500. All the same, these approximations are useful as guides to the way English speech and English writing changed.

But we must use them with care. Quite apart from the

fact that they are only approximations, there is also the important point that the actual *rate of change* was different in different echelons of society. As we are focusing on written English in this book—after all, we are looking at the story of spelling generally and of English in particular—our survey of how English developed is unavoidably skewed in favor of the language of the literate and educated classes of society, who by the dawn of the era of modern English still represented only about five percent of the population.

As well as acknowledging that our survey is inevitably biased in this way, we need to bear in mind that in *rural areas* the rate of change of spoken language (written language was not an issue because most people couldn't write) was much slower than in educated circles.

We make jokes today about rural people speaking of such very plain things as mangel-wurzels in guttural rural accents, and in fact in the 1970s there was indeed a British pop group called The Wurzels that enjoyed some fame for its raunchy, bawdy, and rather cheeky songs about rustic life and haystacks. The Wurzels sang in a rural dialect which was basically Anglo-Saxon in sound if not *entirely* in vocabulary. The very fact that people living urban lives like to see the countryside as a place of earthy satisfactions and uninhibited assignations shows something of a yearning for the supposed traditional and unchanged life of the rural community. The supposed earthiness of country dwellers has probably to some extent always been a myth, because for much of the time since the Anglo-Saxon invasion, country people have been far too preoccupied with staying fed, warm, and free of disease to be quite as raunchy as some might wish to think they are. Nonetheless, the idea that rural people *spoke* in a different way from urban people had a good deal of truth in it until fairly recently—say, the past fifty years or so—when television has transformed rural life, and improved communications and prosperity have meant that if country people *are* going to be raunchy, it is more likely to be in the back of a Range Rover than in a haystack.

Certainly, during the Middle English period, and even during the modern period until the early twentieth century, when radio began to make its influence felt, the countryside was indeed something of a linguistic museum. In rural areas—and especially when communications were poor—older language habits lasted much longer than in heavily populated urban centers.

We can be fairly sure, for instance, that even by the "end" of the Middle English period, there were people living in country areas whose language was fairly close to the English spoken in the days of King Alfred. Shakespeare knew this: In his play *King Lear* he has the good Earl of Kent disguise himself as a rustic yeoman whose language and vocabulary are substantially modernized Anglo-Saxon (that is, modernized in Shakespeare's day). And some Anglo-Saxon words that became obsolete in towns and cities persisted until much later in the countryside.

The nineteenth-century writer Thomas Hardy was a keen observer of life in his native district of Dorset; he called it "Wessex." His novel *The Woodlanders* (1887), set in the countryside of the mid–nineteenth century, is—like most of his stories—largely about the clash between untrustworthy urban sophistication and rural naivete. With Hardy's usual pessimistic view of life and low opinion of rustic simpletons, the smooth-talking, unreliable, urban doctor who comes to sojourn in the sticks gets the girl, while the honest, sincere country hero is left—literally—out in the rain, where he catches a chill and soon afterward dies. It is not a very cheerful book.

Hardy has one of the characters, a rustic old lady, speak a dialect that is more or less nineteenth-century English but includes the word *ich* for "I." In Anglo-Saxon, *ic* meant "I," rather as in modern German the word for "I" is *ich*. Hardy heard *ich* being spoken (in the book the old lady actually says *'ch*). In 1889 he commented that he had heard *ich* in the countryside but observed that it was dying out rapidly.

Yet we don't need to confine ourselves to the works of Shakespeare or Thomas Hardy to hear Anglo-Saxon being spoken many centuries after the Anglo-Saxon period. Anglo-Saxon is still enshrined in the short, everyday words that make up much of our everyday conversation— especially when we are in a bad mood. Rather than spelling out this point in too much detail, I would simply say that all of the short rude words we use in English are

Anglo-Saxon in derivation and the ruder the word is, the more Anglo-Saxon it sounds.

During the century from 1400 to 1500, the days of England being home to two languages—Middle English and Norman French—finally came to an end. Norman French faded away at last as a principal language in England, even though an ability to speak Norman French (and increasingly Parisian French) continued to be a prized ability of educated people.

Meanwhile, three major changes that began to occur at various times during the century wound up having a massive effect on English. The cumulative effect was that the language changed completely.

Even by the end of the fifteenth century, English was in many respects very different from how it was at the start. These changes help to explain why Chaucer's English looks like—and really is—a different language compared with the English that prevailed at the very beginning of the modern English period, only about 120 years after Chaucer was writing.

The *first* major change was a widespread and radical series of alterations in how English vowels were pronounced. Known by scholars of the history of English as the Great Vowel Shift, it affected the seven "long" vowels of English and changed their pronunciation forever.

Scholars do not entirely agree on why the Great Vowel Shift happened. The most convincing argument seems to be that after the massive contribution Norman French had made to English, English was finding its feet again and settling down, during which time some small changes in vowel pronunciation took place by a kind of natural process. Once these changes had occurred, other vowels had to be changed by a sort of consensus on the part of users of the language, in order that vowels could "keep their distance" from their neighbor and avoid confusion as to what words meant.

The linguistic historian David Crystal has devised a sentence to illustrate the vowel changes in the Great Vowel Shift: "**So** it is **time** to **see** the **shoes** on the **same feet now.**" The words in bold contain the vowel sounds that resulted from the Great Vowel Shift. *Before* the Shift the word "so" was pronounced like "saw," "time" like "team," "see" like "say," "shoes" like "shows," "same" like *sarm*, "feet" like "fate," and "now" like *noo*. Chaucer, for example, in the first line of his General Prologue to *The Canterbury Tales*, wrote *shoures* (pronounced in his day something like *shoorers*) where we would write "showers." The spellings of words like *shoures* began to change to harmonize more with the new pronunciation.

The effect of the Great Vowel Shift was major and overwhelming. By the end of the fifteenth century the process was close to complete, and English sounded very different from how it had sounded a century or so earlier. The pronunciation of many other words used in Chaucer's day also changed. As for spelling, it gradually emerged from its state of flux and was soon on the way to enjoying a reasonably standardized form once more—something it hadn't enjoyed since the days of the West Saxon spelling standard.

For example, Chaucer had written *the droghte of march* because he had *said* something like *drocht* (the Anglo-Saxon word had been *drugaþ*), but by the late sixteenth century this word was being pronounced much more like the modern "drought," with the guttural consonant sound by then almost completely absent or only a faint echo of what it had been. Similarly, a word like "night," pronounced by Chaucer something like "nicht" (the Anglo-Saxon word was *niht*, probably also pronounced "nicht"), was by the late sixteenth century being pronounced much as it is today.

But the English spelling system had at last become reasonably fixed again, which explains why in modern English spelling we are lumbered with hundreds of words—such as "drought," "night," and our old friends "cough," "plough," "bough," "ought," and so on—that basically preserve the Anglo-Saxon and early Middle English pronunciation today, at least 600 years since the words were pronounced as they are spelled. Schoolchildren and nonnatives learning to read and write English must unfortunately pay the price and have to learn these singularly irrelevant and ultimately silly spellings. It is some consolation, though not much, to reflect that at least the spellings remind us how the words were pronounced in the Middle Ages and earlier.

The *second* major change that came over the English

language at this time started to occur toward the end of the fifteenth century, at around the time when the modern English period started. This change, which grew and grew in importance during the sixteenth and seventeenth centuries, was that spoken English and written English alike were profoundly influenced by the Renaissance: the enormous revival of interest in the civilizations of ancient Greece and Rome.

The massive surge of interest in the two great civilizations that had flowered in the ancient world was far from being something that happened only in England. It was a Europe-wide phenomenon that changed European civilization forever. Educated people throughout Europe who had a modest knowledge of Latin and a smattering of ancient Greek took the trouble to master Latin if they could and to increase their knowledge of Greek. Just as, during the thirteenth century in England, people had needed to learn Norman French if they wanted to be taken seriously in society and in the world of learning, so from about 1450 onward (the situation lasted for at least 300 years) knowing Latin—and to a lesser extent Greek—was essential for anyone who wanted to be seen as educated. Merely being able to read and write English simply did not cut the mustard.

Toward the end of the fifteenth century, many educated English speakers started to feel that their own language (even, we might add, with all the borrowings from French and Latin during the Middle English period) did not possess the words needed to do justice to the new quality, breadth, and cosmopolitan nature of their think-ing. "Our language is so rusty," the poet John Skelton lamented at the start of his poem "Phyllyp Sparowe" ("Philip Sparrow" in modern spelling), written around 1504. At the time, "rusty" had not yet acquired its modern figurative meaning based on the idea of the physical dete-rioration that occurs when something made of iron or steel rusts. Skelton meant that English was "rustic" in the sense of being primitive and inadequate to express the new, intellectually ambitious ideas that were drifting into the mental firmament.

Because of this, English entered an extraordinary pe-riod when the language absorbed Latin words (and Greek words, though not to so great an extent) as a thirsty man drinks water. Let's remind ourselves, incidentally, that at this point in the history of English, the language was spo-ken only in England. The population of Britain in 1500 was only a little over three million, so fewer people spoke English then than the number of people (about five mil-lion) who speak Finnish today.

The curious thing was that many of these borrowings from Latin had in fact *already been borrowed by English* during the Middle English period, but through the medium of Norman French. In many instances, a Latin word that two centuries earlier had been borrowed by Norman French and then taken from Norman French into English was now borrowed by English directly from Latin. For example, the Latin adjective *pauper,* meaning "poor," was borrowed lock, stock, and barrel by English but was converted during this period into a *noun*. Yet English had already, in the Middle English period, borrowed the Norman French word *povre*, itself derived from the Latin *pauper*. However, English had wound up spelling the word as "poor," and using it as an adjective.

Another example is the Latin word *blasphemare*, which meant "to insult that which should be held as sacred." This word had during the Middle English period been borrowed by English, via Norman French, to give the word "blame." In the fifteenth century, however, the original Latin word was borrowed directly by English to mean exactly what it meant in Latin.

The spelling of the borrowed words was interesting. In principle, the Norman French borrowings and the direct-from-Latin borrowings followed the usual English spelling procedure for borrowed words; that is, they more or less retained their original spellings from the languages from which they were borrowed. But things didn't always work as smoothly as this. Often, when the connection between the direct-from-Latin borrowing and the via–Norman French borrowing was very obvious to English writers, the natural process of *analogy* (or *blending*) came into play—which, in linguistic terms, means the modification of a word to imitate patterns in others. Analogy happens in modern English, too; "motel" (from "motor" and "hotel") and "skyjack" (from "sky" and "hijack") are examples.

During the fifteenth and sixteenth centuries the process of analogy led to changes in the spelling of the

Norman French borrowing along the lines of the direct-from-Latin borrowing. For example, from the Latin participle *perfectum* (which means "completed"), Norman French derived an adjective that passed into Middle English as a word spelled as *perfit* or *parfit*, meaning "properly finished" or "perfect." But the subsequent Renaissance borrowing of the same word *perfectum* direct from Latin, with a change of word-ending to give the English word "perfection," drew attention to the discrepancy between the spellings of "perfection" and *perfit* or *parfit*. As a result, these two Middle English words with varying spellings were modified into a new word in modern English that had only one spelling: "perfect." Not only was the *spelling* of the borrowed Norman French word radically affected by analogy with the direct-from-Latin borrowing, but also the way it was *pronounced*.

This process of analogy radically affected the spelling and pronunciation of many other Middle English words that had been borrowed from Norman French, as many thousands of words were borrowed direct from Latin during the fifteenth and sixteenth centuries. It was a period when the way English was pronounced went through something of a state of transition—as it had been in, really, ever since Anglo-Saxon days. Because of this, many Middle English words that had been borrowed from Norman French not only lost their Middle English *spellings* due to a subsequent direct-from-Latin borrowing in the Renaissance period, but also lost their Middle English *pronunciations* due to the spelling-pronunciation effect that we have already encountered.

Of course, once you take away a word's spelling and also its pronunciation you aren't left with anything except its meaning, and if another word now bears the duty of conveying the meaning, you aren't left with anything at all. Just a few of the many thousands of Middle English words that vanished from the English language during the Renaissance as a result of direct-from-Latin borrowings were as follows:

Original Middle English word borrowed from Norman French	Modern English word borrowed from Latin
assoil	absolve
amonest	admonish
caitif	captive
cors	corpse
descryve	describe
olifaunt	elephant
faucon	falcon
langage	language
peynture	picture
trone	throne

The sweeping extent of these abandoned Norman French borrowings used in Middle English and their replacement by Latin-derived words is another key factor that helps to explain why Geoffrey Chaucer's English seems remote to us today, even though it looks much more modern than Anglo-Saxon does. A highly educated courtier, Chaucer was fluent in French. His writing, in English, makes particularly extensive use of borrowings from French. But as we have seen, many of these borrowings changed their spelling and pronunciation within two centuries after he was writing.

The result of the Romance borrowings into Middle English (from Norman and Parisian French) and later Latin borrowings during the Renaissance period is that today's English is, as we've seen, composed of about forty percent Latin-derived vocabulary. Interestingly, educated English people were aware of the impact of the Romance borrowings even as they were happening. Shakespeare was acutely conscious of the borrowings and played a role in popularizing many of them while also utilizing the expressive potential of the Germanic element of English to a wondrous extent—as with the rustic scenes in *King Lear*.

The *third* major change that started to make itself felt during the last two decades of the fifteenth century—and which would gradually grow in importance until it became perhaps the most significant factor of all in the development of English spelling after the Middle English period—was the introduction of printing. The first printing press in Britain was set up in Westminster, London, in 1476 by William Caxton.

Just as the Norman invasion did not immediately change the nature of the spoken and written English language, Caxton's first printing press did not immediately affect the nature of written English. In fact, printing initially did more to promote the *lack* of a spelling standard than to create one. The earliest printed books produced in England at the end of the fifteenth century are of poor quality and show no particular interest on the part of the printer in taking responsibility for helping develop a standardized way of spelling.

Today this contribution is taken for granted to such an extent that writers who can't spell very well regard the publishing process as their best protection against any of their work being printed with spelling mistakes in it. In fact, printing today plays such a vigorous role in promoting the accepted spelling convention of the English language that when a writer wants to include deliberately *incorrect* spellings, special instructions have to be given so that they are not automatically corrected.

Today, scholars of the history of English believe that printing did not really start to have a major impact on helping to create a standardized convention in English spelling until about 1550; that is, until about seventy years after printing had first been introduced. Why was this? Partly, it appears, because many of the first printers were not fitted by background or outlook for their role of linguistic reformer.

In principle, Caxton himself should have been an exception to this rule. Born in Kent around 1422 (the precise year is unknown), he had only a rudimentary schooling during the 1430s. In 1446 he moved to the town of Bruges in the Low Countries and became involved in the textile industry. An entrepreneurial man by nature, he bettered himself quickly while abroad and became prosperous. He was drawn to printing in his late forties because he had seen the commercial potential of the new technology, which could obviously produce copies of books far more cheaply and rapidly than the current system, which involved copying a manuscript by hand.

Caxton became a wealthy man and attained a position of leadership among Englishmen in the Low Countries who liked to call themselves "merchant adventurers." In 1471 he went to Cologne in Germany to learn the art of printing. He returned to Bruges in 1472, where he set up a press with a Flemish calligrapher named Collard Mansion.

Even before Caxton went to Cologne he had become deeply interested in literature. In March 1469 he had begun to translate from the French a book known as *Recueil des Histoires de Troye* (*Collection of Stories about Troy*). Despite Caxton's interest in the project he found it hard going and often laid it aside, but by the autumn of 1471 he had completed the task. Next, he wanted to sell copies of his translation. In the epilogue of Book III of his completed translation, Caxton tells us how his "pen became worn, his hand weary, his eye dimmed" with copying the book and that the monotony of this labor led him to set himself to learning how to print. Whether or not this is a true account of what happened is far from certain. Why should a prosperous businessman—such as Caxton was by 1470—suddenly want to bother himself with making copies of a book he appears to have translated into English purely for intellectual pleasure? It is possible that Caxton's comments are a sort of medieval equivalent of a press release.

Still, no one could doubt the importance and usefulness of the new technology of printing. Not that the technology was really that new; what was innovative was its sudden widespread use in Europe. (Printing was an art that had originally been invented by the Chinese, who were, however, not motivated to do much with it because of the nature of their writing system.)

Johannes Gutenberg, as far as is known, set up the first printing press in Europe in around 1450 in the town of Mainz. Printing quickly became an exciting new technology with plenty of buzz attached, and Caxton wanted in on it. Having spent two years in Cologne, he returned to Bruges in 1472 and set up a press with his colleague Collard Mansion. It was there in Bruges that Caxton's translation was published under the English title *Recuyell of the Historyes of Troye* (*Recuyell* is a now-obsolete Middle English word meaning "collection" in modern English; it is a typical example of a borrowing from French that didn't survive into modern English).

Caxton's book was the first ever printed in the English language. It is far from exemplary in the quality of its spelling, with many words spelled in different ways within

the work. Still, it sold very well in England, though probably as much for the novelty of the technology as for the
quality of the translation.

The success of his first book in English encouraged
Caxton to return to England toward the end of 1476,
where he established a press at Westminster. After his return to his native land he devoted himself to writing and
printing. His books were popular with wealthy patrons,
and during the next fifteen years he made a great success
of his printing venture. He also devoted himself to translating many books from French and Latin into English,
and by the time of his death in 1491 he had published
about a hundred works covering most branches of literature: stories, poetry (he published *The Canterbury Tales*),
biography, drama, and pretty well anything else that
caught his fancy.

Yet despite Caxton's energetic launch of the printing
industry in Britain and his keen interest in literature, his
work contributed little to the establishment of a standardized spelling system for the English language. The main
reason was that Caxton saw himself as a commercial merchant, selling printed books, rather than as a linguistic reformer. His printing shop in Westminster was mainly a
bookshop, the press itself really being an adjunct brought
into play to supply multiple copies of a popular work at
prices that were much more competitive than those that
could be offered by shops selling handwritten manuscripts
at great expense. Furthermore, much of the machinery
Caxton used at Westminster was imported along with

foreign compositors who knew how to use it. These compositors, unlike the highly literate English scribes, had no talent for regularizing the spelling of the material they set up in type.

Caxton himself did not take a great deal of care over the quality of spelling in the books his compositors produced. Besides, his years abroad had left him out of touch with the spelling developments that had occurred toward the end of the fifteenth century, and he was not particularly interested in those developments anyway. His own spelling reflects the spelling he learned as a boy in the early part of the century, when English was still Middle English and a different language from what was coming into being by around 1500.

The spellings in Caxton's books are extremely inconsistent, and he often haphazardly uses spellings from the languages from which he was translating. Still, some of these have stuck, such as his spelling of the word "ghost." Until the end of the fifteenth century it had been spelled in English as *gost*, but Caxton borrowed the spelling from Dutch, where the word began with the letters *gh*. This explains why we still spell "ghost" with an *h* at the beginning that has no purpose whatsoever—unless to scare children by making ghostly noises that sound as if they ought to have quite a few *H*'s in them.

On Caxton's death in 1491 his press was taken over by his assistant, Wynkyn de Worde, with the assistance of a printer named Richard Pynson. However, de Worde came from the French region of Alsace-Lorraine and Pynson was Norman French by birth; English was not even their mother tongue. Neither of these men could have been expected to make a major contribution toward the evolution of a standard for English spelling, and they didn't. But they did tend to prefer English compositors to foreign ones, which was a step in the right direction.

The truth of the matter is that Caxton, de Worde, Pynson, and other early printers working in the late fifteenth and early sixteenth centuries were essentially operating outside the mainstream tradition of the highly literate and educated scribes who mainly wrote English in monasteries. For us today, it is difficult to imagine the situation in the early years of printing where spellings in books varied not only from one book to another, but even from one page or paragraph to another within the same book.

However, matters began to change as the sixteenth century advanced. Printers became more aware of their responsibilities in setting a standard for spelling. Many printers consequently took a profound interest in the work of professional scribes and even hired scribes to check over type that had been set and was ready to print, rather like hiring a modern proofreader.

This significant change in attitude meant that the printing houses adopted the spelling practices of scribes and of the shops which produced multiple copies of handwritten manuscripts. The consistency of the spelling of printed books dramatically improved, and by around 1550 their consistency of spelling was about as good as that found in manuscripts.

But that is to jump ahead a little. The crucial century, from 1400 to 1500, was the one when English went through its revolutionary changes stemming from the three factors already mentioned. By around 1500 the English language had taken on a completely new incarnation—a language we can justifiably call modern English—and it was a world away from what had been spoken only a century before. When you read anything from about 1500 onward, it looks very obviously like the English we speak today, and those differences that there are stem more from irregularities in the spelling than from major differences in the language from the English of the twenty-first century. Of course, early modern English did not contain the plethora of borrowings that have made English today what it is. But it is still recognizably the same language, and calling it modern English does not seem unreasonable. The revolution was complete, and English had changed forever.

The hundred years from around 1550 to 1650 saw the gradual acceptance by most printers of the notion that a spelling convention *ought* to exist, and they played a major role—perhaps *the* major role—in enforcing it. But while printers became increasingly committed to this new role, the contribution they could make to the consistency of spelling was hampered by the fact that the actual spelling of written English was still evolving during these one hundred years.

A particular problem was that while educated people increasingly recognized the practical necessity for printed writing to demonstrate consistent spelling, they did not recognize the same level of necessity for the spelling in their *private* writings. This problem is particularly seen in private writings during the reign of Queen Elizabeth I, who ruled England from 1558 to 1603.

Elizabeth's reign covered perhaps the greatest-ever period of English literature. It saw the writing and performance of most of Shakespeare's plays, as well as the creation of many works by other great writers. Yet even the greatest writers of the time did not seem to care particularly about how consistent their spelling was. From looking at the spelling in private letters and documents of the period and contrasting it with the spelling in printed works, there seems to be a tension between printers and writers, with printers trying to find ways of establishing a standard and writers not caring whether there was such a thing.

The situation wasn't helped by the fact that although literacy rates were improving (most Elizabethan gentry were literate and most social groups above peasants had an average of about twenty percent literacy), grammar-school education for boys aged ten or older was mainly concerned with the study of the grammar of *Latin* rather than English. Grammar schools were called that because of the Latin grammar the boys were studying. Primary education—directed at children up to the age of about ten—tended to focus on the reading and writing of English. The quality of this education, where available, varied considerably. Up to around 1550, even those teachers who were trying to teach their young charges to read and write their mother tongue were hampered by the absence of textbooks in English and by the lack of any obvious spelling standard. The situation improved to some extent later during the sixteenth century, but even by around 1600 the most literate and educated people in Britain thought it was perfectly fine to spell the same word in different ways even within the same letter or manuscript. To take just one example, the modern word "pity" was routinely spelled during the Elizabethan era in all of the following forms, and more besides: "pity," "pyty," "pitie," "pytie," "pittie," and "pyttye." What about Shakespeare himself? We don't know how the greatest writer of all time actually spelled because no manuscripts definitely written by him survive, but he certainly spelled his own name in at least two different ways in his will—"Shakspere" and "Shakspeare"—and very likely he spelled it in other ways elsewhere.

Elizabethans preferred certain spellings of a particular word, but the notion that there should be just one way for a particular word to be spelled was not really part of the mind-set of the Elizabethans. Still, we can't say they spelled badly, as there was no standard convention for them to follow. But we can say they spelled *inconsistently,* and

we can argue that any writing system with a range of varying spellings cannot possibly be as efficient for communicating as a system where there is only one accepted
spelling and everything else is considered substandard.

As for printers, many seemed to have wanted to en-
courage and promote the development of a standardized
form of spelling. However, they weren't helped in this respect by the nature of the printing machinery they used.
During the first two centuries of printing, the comparatively primitive machinery available did not allow for fine
adjustments in the spacing between words. These adjustments were used later to facilitate the process of type justification, whereby all the lines on a printed page end
at precisely the same place on the right-hand margin.
Instead of this, early printing tended to end at slightly
different places and so the creation of a clear and neat
right-hand margin was difficult. Printers, despite their increasing commitment to creating a spelling standard, were
also concerned about the appearance of their printed pages.
Many of them dealt with the margin problem by the "logical" means of adding letters to words where doing so
made a line "neater" in the sense of being more similar in
length to the ones above and below.

The spelling, for example, of the famous King James
Bible published in 1611 is in fact no more uniform than the
spelling in Shakespeare's First Folio, printed in 1623 and
containing all of his plays except *Pericles*. Both these immortal productions of the early seventeenth century, glit-
tering with language that deserves to be read for as long as

humankind exists, are spelled in a variety of inconsistent ways—though this is usually lost on people who study Shakespeare today, as his spellings are routinely modernized.

One modern commentator on early-seventeenth-century spelling, Alfred Pollard, has remarked that the *only* consistency is that the form was always preferred which suited the spacing. But by around 1630 the problem was already starting to recede as printers finally began to allow their determination to help establish a spelling standard overcome their desire to make the ends of their lines look neat. The two Authorized Versions of the Bible, published in 1629 and 1638, feature much more consistent spelling.

Chapter 9

───

The First Dictionaries

And let a scholar all Earth's volumes carry, he will be but a walking dictionary.

—George Chapman,
Teares of Peace (1609)

OW can we get a good idea of the state of English spelling at the start of the seventeenth century? I couldn't think of a better way than to visit the Rare Books section of the British Library in London and consult a tiny but profoundly revealing book: *A Table Alphabeticall*.

One of the very first dictionaries of English ever published, *A Table Alphabeticall* was first published in 1603 and went through several editions. The edition I consulted for *Spellbound* was the third, published in 1613; I wanted to see an edition published when the *Table* was established as a successful publication and with initial printers' errors corrected. Successive editions of the book increased the number of words: The third edition has in excess of 1,000 words more than the first.

Considering that we are used to dictionaries being

bulky things we have to heave down from shelves, the *Table* is reassuringly light. It weighs about the same as a mobile phone and is not much bigger, being just under four inches long, barely three inches wide, less than half an inch thick, and just over 160 pages in length. In fact, when I was given the book by the assistant at the British Library after I'd waited in line in the Rare Books section for about twenty minutes, I looked at what she had given me and said, "Is this it?" She gave me an apologetic nod and several of the bearded people in the line behind me ventured a laugh: not a sound you hear very much in the Rare Books section of the British Library.

As you might imagine from the fact that *A Table Alphabeticall* is dimensionally challenged, it does not contain an enormous number of words. In fact, it lists only about 4,000, and while the vocabulary of English in 1603 was not as large as it is today, these words would only have been a small proportion of the total vocabulary of early-seventeenth-century English. But the dictionary-maker was not trying to produce a comprehensive dictionary but rather one that focused on words that were difficult to spell. The listings themselves are very basic: The word is given, followed by a brief phrase defining it.

The purpose of the *Table* is stated very clearly on the title page (here I use the precise spellings of the third edition, but have modernized the lowercase *s*):

A Table Alphabeticall, contayning and teaching the true writing and vnderstanding of hard vsuall English words, borrowed from the Hebrew, Greeke, Latin or French &c

With the Interpretation thereof by plaine English words, gathered for the benefit and help of all vnskilfull persons.

Whereby they may the more easily and better vnderstand many hard English words, which they shall heare or read in Scriptures, Sermons, or else where and also be made able to vse the same aptly themselves.

The Latin motto quoted lower down on the title page sums up the entire rationale of this worthy enterprise, with a rather loose English translation provided:

Legere, & non intelligere, neglegere est
As good not to read, as not to understand

In 1613, just like today, you didn't publish a book unless you were confident of making money from it, which meant you had to be confident you would find a readership. Writing a book in the first place was (and is) hard work, printing it was a speculative game, and these were days when all you could really do to promote your book was to put up a few placards in public places to advertise where the book could be bought, and hope for the best. So the author, who is not mentioned by name in the *Table* but was in fact one Robert Cawdrey, must have been confident that the publication would sell. The printer very likely shared his confidence: Printers of the time frequently shared some of the risk of a publication. The title page states the books have been "Printed by *T.S.* for *Edmund Weauer*, and are to be sold at his shop at the great North dore of Paules Church, 1613." (This means the *old* church of St. Paul's, by the way, not the new one, which was built after the original burned down in the Great Fire of London, fifty-three years in the future.) In any event, Cawdrey's book *did* sell, although there is no way of knowing how many copies were printed in each edition, or how many copies the various editions of the book sold altogether.

The *Table* gives the impression of providing its readers with an urgent report from a battlefield where a battle was still being fought. It was the battle for the English language to assert itself as an infinitely subtle and expressive tongue, through borrowings from the great cultures of the past; through new, figurative applications of words that previously had only had concrete and literal meanings; and through the efforts of great writers—when the third edition of the *Table* was published, Shakespeare had only three years left to live and all his sublime works had been written. Ultimately, the battle involved English struggling to earn its laurels as a language that was no less great, and potentially even greater, than the classical tongues that had preceded it.

Cawdrey is plainly aware that his readers may never have used such a book before, because at the end of a section entitled "To the Reader" he gives precise instructions on how to use the little book. Even the spelling in this third edition features some differences from the first edition, published in 1604—an apparently unique copy of which is in the Bodleian Library, Oxford. For example, the word spelled "dore" in 1613 is spelled "doore" in the first edition of 1604. An even more explicit indication of the continuing inconsistency of spelling at the start of the seventeenth century is that the title-page text of the 1604 edition spells "words" as "wordes" in the *first* paragraph and as "words" in the *third* paragraph. But by the 1613 edition the spelling in the first paragraph has been amended to "words."

The helpful instructions to the reader provided in the *Table* are worth quoting in full. They are interesting in themselves, and they also show how, by 1613, English spelling was really not that different from how it is today. Even though many words in the *Table* are nowadays spelled slightly differently, they are still easily readable. In the following, and subsequent, quotations from the book, I have retained the original spelling.

If thou be desirous (gentle Reader) rightly and readily to vnderstand, and to profit by this Table, and such like, then thou must learne the Alphabet, *to wit*, the order of the letters as they stand, perfectly without booke, and where euery Letter standedth: as (b) neere the beginning, (n) about the middest, and (t) towards the end. Now if the word, which thou are desirous to finde, begin with (a) then looke in the beginning of this Table, but if with (v) looke towards the end. Again, if thy word begin with (ca) looke in the beginning of the Letter (c) but if with (cu) then looke toward the end of that Letter. And so of all the rest &c.

Apart from the extremely useful information the *Table* furnishes about the state of spelling in the England of 1613, the book also reveals that many "difficult" English words had not yet acquired the additional, figurative meaning they have acquired since then. For example, the author defines "vndermine" as "grauen, dig under," which suggests that the meaning of gradual or insidious weakening—the one people would usually think of first today—had not yet appeared. "Admission" is defined as "receiving, of leave to enter into a place, access," with no mention of the figurative sense of a concession in an argument or case. And "assumption" is defined as "taking," whereas the modern dominant sense of the word is the figurative one of believing something based on evidence that may be inadequate. Figurative meanings of words deriving from original, literal meanings tend to dominate the literal meanings in modern English.

The following examples show that English spelling around 1613 was already very similar to today's English. The first word listed in the *Table* is "abandon," defined as "call away, or yielde up, to leave or forsake." In other words, apart from the extra *e* on the word "yield," the spellings are exactly as they would be in modern English. The last word listed is "zonet," defined as "circles in the heavens, dividing the world into finite parts." But I think the extra *t* is a printer's error, as the word "zonet" is not found anywhere else, including the *Oxford English Dictionary*.

There are only two other words beginning with *Z* in the *Table*:

> *zenith*, the point of heauen right ouer our heads.
> *zodiack* (g), a circle in the heauen, wherein be placed
> the 12. Signs, and in which the Sunne is moued.

The (g) indicates that the word comes from Greek (as the *Table* explains before providing the list of words).

While the spelling throughout the *Table* is very much like modern English, there are a few exceptions. Words that end with a *c* in modern English spelling are usually spelled with a final *k* after the *c* and sometimes also with an additional *e*; for example, "magic" is spelled as "magicke." (The word "logic," incidentally, is not listed.) Some words whose spelling ends as a consonant in modern English have a doubled consonant in the *Table*—the very word "alphabeticall" is an example—and sometimes the word takes an additional *e*, as with "sunne." The extra *e* is often seen in adverbs; for example, "fragrant" is defined as "sweetely smelling." A final *e* is added to many words that would not take a final *e* in modern spelling; "wood," for instance, is spelled "woode." Finally, words that would be spelled with an *ai* in the middle today are usually spelled with an *ay* in the *Table*; for example, "pertaining" is spelled "pertayning."

The *Table* does reveal, however, that there were some

more substantial differences from modern English. First, there is no letter *j* at all. Words that would begin in modern English with the *j* semivowel—the *j*-sound in James, for example—in modern English are spelled with an initial *i* (which is also used for the usual *i* vowel) and are listed among words beginning with *i*. For instance:

> *iudaisme,* worshipping one God without Christ
> *iudicious,* that hath a good judgement or understanding

Second, the *Table* has the capital *S* written like the English letter, but the lowercase *s* written as ʃ. This letter looks very much like the *f* in the book, which no doubt helps to explain why this kind of lowercase initial *s* was abandoned in subsequent centuries.

Third, there are no listings at all for the letter *U*. Words that would today be spelled with an initial *u* are listed as beginning with a *v*. For example, "vnion," defined as "concord," and "vnsatiable," defined as "not content." The *Table* does use the letter *u* in many words that are employed to explain definitions, but prefers *v* for initial positions. This suggests that Cawdrey did not distinguish between *u* and *v* but more or less used them interchangeably.

There is something utterly charming about the *Table*'s enthusiasm to impart knowledge and the distant echo it provides of a world when the English language was still being forged in the crucible of the Renaissance.

I left the *Table* behind in the Rare Books section of the

British Library with a heavy heart. How agreeable it would have been to walk across to the City of London, find "Edmund Weauer" and Bob Cawdrey at the little bookshop by the north door of old St. Paul's church, and accompany them to a local tavern for an evening of drinking ale, eating saveloys, and talking of the delights and mysteries of the English language! And who knows: If Shakespeare was visiting London that evening on a trip from Stratford, he might even have joined us for a while. "My pieces dramaticall are not much presented by players any more," he might lament. "Forsooth, methinks I am all forgotten. My dramas are not even set in print."

Which, in 1613, they weren't, nor indeed were they three years later, when Shakespeare slipped from this mortal coil. The greatest writer in history died out of print.

From about 1550 onward there is a distinct sense that many educated and literate people were dissatisfied with the way English spelling was going. This dissatisfaction showed itself in a range of publications—including of course the *Table Alphabeticall*—that attempted to set down how the writer thought English should be spelled. There were also spelling books published for children to advise them how to spell properly.

All these books, whether intended for children or for adults, look slightly absurd nowadays because they essentially embody and advocate spellings that were not yet part of a national standard, so different books advocate different spellings, and it is actually entirely common for the same word to be spelled in two or more different ways within the same book.

The problem was that the standard for spelling was evolving during this next crucial century from about 1550 to 1650. By definition, if you try to set down an interim report about something that is still evolving, your report is going to be inaccurate. Of course, the people writing these books were not aware that English spelling was, in fact, evolving toward some kind of standard; as far as they were concerned, they were simply dealing with a highly inconsistent situation and trying their best to make sense of it and to legislate for it.

Printers were gradually becoming aware of their own responsibilities in enshrining consistent spelling. However, their position was quite complicated. On the one hand, they were keen to move toward consistency because this would make it easier for them to do their job. On the other hand, they needed to sell books and so they hardly wanted to use spellings that were not yet popular with readers. This was a time of professional difficulty for printers, many of whom were by now highly conscientious professionals. They wanted to try to contribute toward the development of an English spelling standard, but they also needed to make money.

One historical event which made a definite impact on the consistency of English spelling was the British Civil War. Fought between the Royalists and the Roundheads (the Parliamentary party), it began in 1642 and ended in

1651 with a resounding victory by the Roundheads, who established a monarchless dictatorship of the landed middle classes. This dictatorship was the foundation for British democracy, and even though the "Commonwealth" regime created by Oliver Cromwell was dissolved just two years after his death in 1658, Britain was henceforth a country in which the monarch would have minimal power and Parliament would decide what happened.

The (literal) cut and thrust of the Civil War led to considerable fortunes being made by printers who were able to produce—to very tight time frames—broadsheets giving news about the war to the population. Many rival publications were produced, and because time was at a premium, there was actually an impetus in favor of words being printed in their *shorter* form to reduce the time taken to set the broadsheet in print and to get it out to an eager marketplace.

Half a century or so earlier, printers were more interested in the accurate justification of their lines. Now an opposite kind of force was in play; printers were motivated to make their lines shorter in order to get the publication out more quickly. This had a definite effect on the consistency of English spelling. In particular it tended to reduce the use of a final -*e* and to reduce the number of words that ended with a double consonant. Examples, from just one page of a spelling book entitled *The English Schoole-maister* (published in 1596 by one Edmond Coote) are "beneficiall," "capitall," and "cathedrall," which nowadays are spelled with a single consonant. We have already seen that the word "alphabeticall" was spelled with two final consonants in the editions of Robert Cawdrey's book.

Spelling was adhering much more closely to a standard by the time the British Civil War ended, and the war unquestionably played a part in the evolution of that standard. Another factor, according to Nigel Roche—one of the leading experts in Britain on the history of printing—was that there was a new spirit of inquiry and sharp intellectual endeavor in British culture, which increasingly regarded an inconsistent spelling system as absurd and undignified. As so often in the history of culture, we are dealing less with one specific event that heralded a profound change of attitude and more with a general move to a new mood whose time had come.

In practice, by about the year 1700, the stabilization and standardization of the English spelling system was close to complete. The relatively few changes that have taken place in spelling since then have in fact only affected a small number of words.

For example, since 1700 the word "controul" has become "control," and some words starting with *ph* are now spelled with an initial *f* (such as "phantasy," now of course spelled "fantasy"), though many retain a *ph* at the start. In fact, the *ph* is simply an attempt to render in English letters the Greek letter "phi," which looks like this: Φ and was pronounced something like a very breathy *p*, a bit like the *p*-sound in the English word "uphill."

Other classical borrowings have also been affected by spelling changes since the borrowings were made. For example, the word "economic" was often spelled up until the nineteenth century as "œconomic," as were many other words that had been borrowed by English from Latin via Greek. The letter *œ* was how Latin represented the Greek vowel combination *oi*. Today, some British English words ("oesophagus," for example) still begin with *oe*, which is a modernized form of *œ*—although American English spelling prefers such words to start with a simple *e*, as in "esophagus." But "œconomic" has indeed standardized to "economic," doubtless because this is quite a common word and it was felt that a more ordinary-looking English appearance was more appropriate for it.

For much the same reason, many words that were formerly spelled with an ash (*æ*) are now spelled with *ae*. Other minor developments since 1700 include the loss of a final *-k* from words such as "music" and "comic." The most recent major development in English spelling that affected the actual letters of English was, as we have seen, that *u* and *v* continued to be treated as one letter alphabetically for a long time, even until the 1830s. However, by 1840 at the latest, the letters *u* and *v* were regarded as individual letters and were used as they are today.

There is a general perception among many people who know something of the history of English spelling that Dr. Samuel Johnson's famous *Dictionary of the English Language*, published in 1755 in two volumes—the product of ten years' labor—played a crucial role in helping to fix English spelling. However, the truth of the matter is that by 1755 English spelling was already very fixed and Johnson was therefore essentially setting down a standard that was already substantially completed. Johnson was commissioned by a group of London publishers to create the dictionary. The publishers underwrote this massive project.

Johnson was not a man to do things by halves. The very first page of his *Dictionary* is entirely uncompromising in announcing what he has sought to do:

> A Dictionary of the English language: in which the words are deduced from their originals and illustrated in their different significations by examples from the best writers.

It is not often realized, by people who haven't handled it, that Johnson's *Dictionary* is a mighty work not only at conceptual and practical levels but also at a *physical* level. Its two volumes are each nearly seventeen inches long, eleven inches wide, and just over three inches thick. The volumes are beautifully printed, with two columns on each page: The job of setting the type by hand (which was of course the way things were done at the time) is mind-boggling. Original editions of the *Dictionary* are very much worth viewing if you can get access to one.

Johnson's *Dictionary* is an entirely wonderful publication. Above all, it is infused with an extraordinary enthusiasm for the craft of dictionary-making and, considering how exhausted Johnson often must have been from the work, with an amazing energy. Johnson evidently wrote every definition himself, and his style, urbanity, and wisdom make the *Dictionary* a fascinating read. Furthermore, the impact of the *Dictionary* was massive. For over 150 years after its first publication, Johnson's *Dictionary* was an essential item on every educated Englishman's bookshelf, alongside the Bible and the works of Shakespeare. Yet ultimately its contribution to the history of English spelling lies more in the quality of the writing Johnson brought to the business of dictionary-making rather than to any new direction given to spelling.

Johnson himself was aware of his dilemma as a dictionary-maker who would have preferred his work to reflect a more consistent style of English spelling, but was obliged to set down the way things were rather than the way he wished them to be. This is important to remember because in the sixteenth and early seventeenth centuries there was usually a sense among people who wrote the early, short lists of "hard wordes" and early, brief dictionaries that the dictionary-maker had a right, essentially, to pontificate on how the spelling *ought* to be. For Johnson, a dictionary-maker had no right to pontificate about anything. In his Preface—which exhibits in all their grandeur Johnson's splendid literary style, moral conviction, and intelligent humility—he belittles the role of the dictionary-maker and also, significantly, acknowledges that the dictionary-maker, if doing the job properly, is inevitably relegated to recording usage. As he puts it:

It is the fate of those who toil at the lower employ-
ments of life, to be rather driven by the fear of evil, than
attracted by the prospect of good; to be exposed to cen-
sure, without hope of praise; to be disgraced by miscar-
riage, or punished for neglect, where success would
have been without applause, and diligence without re-
ward.

Among these unhappy mortals is the writer of dictionaries; whom mankind have considered, not as the
pupil, but the slave of science, the pioneer of literature,
doomed only to remove rubbish and clear obstructions
from the paths of Learning and Genius, who press forward to conquest and glory, without bestowing a smile
on the humble drudge that facilitates their progress.
Every other authour may aspire to praise; the lexicographer can only hope to escape reproach, and even this
negative recompense has been yet granted to very few.

I have, not withstanding this discouragement, attempted a dictionary of the English language, which,
while it was employed in the cultivation of every
species of literature, has itself been hitherto neglected,
suffered to spread, under the direction of chance, into
wild exuberance, resigned to the tyranny of time and
fashion, and exposed to the corruptions of ignorance,
and caprices of innovation.

When I took the first survey of my undertaking, I
found our speech copious without order, and energetick
without rules: wherever I turned my view, there was
perplexity to be disentangled, and confusion to be

regulated; choice was to be made out of boundless variety, without any established principle of selection; adulterations were to be detected, without a settled test of purity, and modes of expression to be rejected or received, without the sufferages of any writers of classical reputation or acknowledged authority.

Having therefore no assistance but from general grammar, I applied myself to the perusal of our writers; and noting whatever might be of use to ascertain or illustrate any word or phrase, accumulated in time the materials of a dictionary, which, by degrees, I reduced to method, establishing to myself, in the progress of the work, such rules as experience and analogy suggested to me; experience, which practice and observation were continually increasing; and analogy, which, though in some words obscure, was evident in others.

There is a hilarious episode of the popular British TV comedy *Blackadder* in which the actor Robbie Coltrane plays Dr. Johnson with much gusto, though exuding a personality that is pretty much the opposite of the brilliant but fundamentally humble character suggested in these paragraphs from the Preface. In the episode in question, the great doctor—who has just finished his dictionary after ten years ("Yes, well, I'm a slow reader myself," comments the obtuse Prince of Wales)—is depicted as a pompous literary know-it-all who believes he has the right to pronounce on what correct spelling should be.

Blackadder cunningly flummoxes Dr. Johnson (who is proud that his great work contains every word in the English language) by spontaneously inventing nonexistent words that the great doctor thinks must really exist. Dr. Johnson finally goes off in a flurry of exasperation at discovering that he had forgotten to include the word "sausage" in his dictionary.

So *was* sausage included? The answer is a resounding yes, the word "savsage" being found in the dictionary between "savoy" and "saw." Its definition is: "a roll or ball made commonly of pork or veal, and sometimes of beef, minced very small, with salt and spice; sometimes it is stuffed into the guts of fowls, and sometimes only rolled in flower" ("flower" was used as an alternative spelling of "flour" to spell the finest part of a grain until as late as the early nineteenth century). Since Johnson lived at the time when *u* and *v* were still regarded as the same, interchangeable letter, the word isn't listed according to the modern standard where *u* and *v* are two separate letters and *u* comes before *v*. This episode of *Blackadder* makes for a highly entertaining half-hour, but doesn't do justice to Johnson, who was by all accounts a humble, if thorough, lexicographer, passionately committed to setting down not what he thought the spellings of English should be, but what they actually *were*.

The principle that *usage* should be the defining criterion for any book written about the state of English, the meaning of words, the spelling of words, and so on has been enshrined in British culture since about the eighteenth century and—quite rightly—has been extended to other languages. It has to be observed because, ultimately, a language is bigger than any individual and if any individuals seek to try to impose their own will on it, they are not only doomed to failure but are doing themselves, and scholarship, a great injustice. As Dr. Johnson concedes later in his Preface:

> I have often been obliged to sacrifice uniformity to custom; thus I write, in compliance with a numberless majority, *convey* and *inveigh, deceit* and *receipt, fancy* and *phantom.*

The fact that these words have retained their inconsistencies in their modern spellings shows that Dr. Johnson was absolutely right to follow the fashion of the day, which had already laid down the spelling of these words. Johnson does not tell us what spellings he would have chosen had he *not* been sacrificing uniformity to custom. However, he may have been thinking of spellings that had been used earlier in the century when he was a boy but were now fading from the language: respectively, "convay"/"conveigh," "enveigh," "receit"; "fansie"/"phansy"/ "phansie"; "phantome"/"phantosme." Despite careful investigation, I have not been able to find out what alternative spelling for "deceit" there was in the earlier part of the eighteenth century. Almost a century before the publication of the *Dictionary,* the great English poet John Milton used the spelling "deceit" in his poem *Paradise Lost* (1667), and the spelling seems to have been established in its modern form by then. It is not clear to me why Johnson included this word in his list.

The spelling of Johnson's own Preface, of course, shows just how similar his spelling was to our own. However, Johnson did have an extremely potent influence in one respect: By reflecting and stating the accepted standard of *public* spelling (that is, the spellings already widely used by printers), the *Dictionary* also became the accepted standard for *private* spelling during the late eighteenth and nineteenth centuries. After the publication of the *Dictionary,* the great variations in the spelling of private correspondence that are so noticeable in the sixteenth and seventeenth centuries faded dramatically.

When you remember that the *Dictionary* was set purely using manual printing techniques, the scale of the work and the effort involved in producing it seems extraordinary, especially as Johnson does not shrink from using Anglo-Saxon letters to spell out original Anglo-Saxon sources, and also presents many Middle English words in their original spellings. The scholarship of his *Dictionary* is essentially mind-blowing, and puts us all to shame with our word processors, font sets, Internet research, and all the other tools of modern scholarship which mean that scholars need no longer labor in drudgery.

There are altogether 42,773 definitions in Johnson's

Dictionary, supported by a total of 110,000 quotations.
Johnson was aided by six, or sometimes seven, assistants
who worked with him in the garret of his house in Gough
Square off Fleet Street. Their task was to copy the passages from various literary sources that Johnson had
marked up as illustrations for his definitions. It was a
technique that Johnson probably did not pioneer but
which was certainly extensively used and implicitly became an essential tool in the work of any future committed lexicographer.

While we must admit the enormous importance and
utility of Johnson's dictionary, his book is by no means an
immaculate conception. Thorough and inspired it may be,
but it is also sometimes rather silly. For one thing, many of
the words he defines are artificial words, based closely on
Latin roots, and were probably barely used even in his
own day.

As for his definitions, many of them are quite self-
indulgent and so unhelpful he would have been better off
rewriting them. For example, he defines a "cough" as "a
convulsion of the lungs, vellicated by some sharp serosity."
So now we know. He defines a "fish" very feebly as "an animal that inhabits the water" (many other types of creatures do that aren't fishes) and he defines a "hiccough" (a
word that is still spelled this way today, but more often
nowadays as "hiccup") rather absurdly as "to sob with con-
vulsions of the stomach." He defines a "lexicographer" as
"a maker of dictionaries, a harmless drudge that busies

SPELLBOUND

himself in tracing the original, and detailing the significa-
tion of words," but this is really Johnson telling us about
himself (and implying that women cannot be lexicogra-
phers) rather than informing us what the word "lexicographer" means. A nonnative speaker reading the *Dictionary*
might think that "harmless drudge" is a synonym for "lexicographer," which of course it isn't.

Other definitions are just plain rude. For example, he
defines "oats" as "a grain, which in England is generally
given to horses, but in Scotland supports the people." I am
sure the tens of thousands of impoverished Scottish children of the eighteenth and nineteenth centuries, with little to eat but porridge, and not often much of that, would
have found that definition highly amusing. It's surprising
the ghost of William Wallace didn't visit Johnson by night
and toss a caber at him.

Yet Johnson was also thorough and intensely dedicated
to his huge task. He gives, for example, 134 different definitions for the verb "to take." Sometimes his definitions
are poetic ("nightmare" is defined as "a morbid oppression
in the night, resembling the pressure of weight upon the
breast") and at other times admirably strong and uncompromising ("cant" is "high-sounding language unsup-
ported by dignity of thought").

In effect, Johnson's *Dictionary* is not only a setting-in-
stone of English spelling in 1755, but—as the writer Kate
Chisholm pointed out in 2005 in an article about Dr.
Johnson's *Dictionary*—it also provides:

[259]

[A] snapshot of social life in Britain in the mid-eighteenth century as it emerged from a rural, superstitious, uncommercial world to one in which urban values and pursuits prevailed...

Johnson's feat was the scholarly equivalent of climbing Everest, or walking to the Pole: an adventure, an exploration and a defiant attempt at immortality. It was not the first English dictionary to appear in print, but it became the model for all that followed. Within ten years it turned Johnson into a celebrity, who was gossiped about daily in the newspapers. When he died in 1784, there was an unseemly rush by biographers wishing to cash in on his fame, culminating in 1791 with Boswell's *Life*.

Today, copies of Johnson's *Dictionary* are a rarity and good-quality copies are extremely valuable. Johnson himself never made much money from his *Dictionary*. He received 1,500 guineas for it—the equivalent of around £150,000 (or $250,000) today—but by the time he had supported himself over the ten years it took to write it and paid his assistants, he would have done better financially growing oats.

By the beginning of the nineteenth century there was an increasing recognition that a language was too vast an entity for one man's scholarship to encapsulate it, no matter how devoted the man might be to the task. Johnson was the last lexicographer in Britain to attempt the job himself. In the United States, the last dictionary-maker to attempt the big job alone was Noah Webster, whose surname is nowadays effectively a brand signifying the most widely respected dictionary of American English.

Webster was born in 1758 in West Hartford, Connecticut. He entered Yale University in 1774, interrupted his studies briefly to fight in the Revolutionary War, and graduated in 1778. On graduation Webster taught in a school in Goshen, New York, did clerical work, and studied law. He was admitted to the bar in 1781.

While he was teaching in Goshen, Webster became dissatisfied with texts for children that were written without what he regarded as a proper recognition of American culture. This led him to begin his lifelong attempts to promote a distinctively American education. His first step in this direction was the preparation of what he called *A Grammatical Institute of the English Language*, which he intended to be a comprehensive study of the English language but from the point of view of the needs of Americans. The first part of his study he named *The American Spelling Book* (1783): the famed "Blue-Backed Speller" which is so familiar in the United States. This spelling book has never been out of print. It provided much of Webster's income for the remainder of his life, and it has been estimated to have sold as many as 100,000,000 copies or even more.

A grammar (1784) and a reader (1785) completed the *Institute*. The grammar book was based on Webster's deeply held belief that "grammar is founded on language, and not language on grammar"—meaning that usage was what really mattered. Although Webster did not always follow this principle himself and often relied on analogy, special pleading, and false etymology, his inconsistencies were really no greater than those of his English contemporaries. His reader consisted principally of extracts from American writing chosen to promote democratic ideals and responsible moral and political conduct. The Declaration of Independence had been signed in 1776, and America had won its War of Independence in 1783, the same year when *The American Spelling Book* was first published. A new Constitution was created in 1787, ratified in 1788, and took effect in 1789. Chosen, as it were, by destiny and the fact of being born at just the right time, Webster grasped his fate as the arbiter of the English of the newly independent nation. He called American English "Federal English" and contrasted it with London English, which he depicted as full of affectation and falsehood. Webster saw moral, political, and linguistic values as being closely bound up with one another, and maybe he was right.

As inheritors of the language of Britain—their former oppressor—the citizens of the now-independent United States could hardly avoid harboring resentment toward the language that was their legacy. This resentment, had it been more widespread, might have turned into some concrete action. There was talk immediately after the war of the new independent nation abandoning English completely and replacing it with classical Greek. But this was hardly a practical solution, as people—especially wealthy landowners, which most of the American leaders were—do not abandon their mother tongue very readily. No, the Americans stuck with English, but at least they could make it *their* English.

Given the strength of anti-British feeling in the United States at this time—a feeling that perhaps has not mellowed since then quite as much as British political leaders like to think when they make their fawning visits to the White House—it is rather surprising that the United States retained the entire heritage of the English language to such a comprehensive extent. The severing of political links with Britain seemed the ideal opportunity for the new nation to say, in effect, "We will retain your accursed language, for we are too busy building this great country into one that is even greater to learn a new language, but we will spell it completely differently. We will spell it how it should be spelled and not in this absurd fashion that is the legacy of your hybrid past."

And yet this did not happen. Not only did British English spelling continue, by and large, to be the spelling used in the United States, but the American language continued to be much the same as British English: The differences between the two languages are very minor at a structural level. The differences in terms of vocabulary are more substantial, but ultimately superficial in that they do not prevent the American and British versions of English being unquestionably the same language.

Very likely the American and British forms of English

would have diverged more if there had been fewer continuing cultural connections between the United States and Britain. America became independent comparatively recently, shortly before the start of the nineteenth century: a century that was replete with transatlantic communication between the United States and Britain. Where two regions using the same language are separated geographically but continue to maintain strong cultural links and communications, the language tends to remain much the same in both regions. Where this is not the case, the languages will start to diverge, sometimes to the extent that they become mutually incomprehensible.

For example, when Dutch settlers (the Boers) first went to South Africa in 1652, the great distance from the Netherlands and the poor communications of the time across such distances meant that most of them lost contact with the Netherlands entirely. They began by speaking Dutch, but their language gradually evolved into a different form—a sort of simplified Dutch that contained many loanwords from neighboring African languages. The language their descendants speak today—Afrikaans—is still close enough to Dutch to be reasonably comprehensible to a Dutch speaker, but it is certainly a different language, structurally as well as in much of the vocabulary.

The main reason why American English spelling never underwent a massive spelling reform after the United States won its independence appears to be the same reason no other comprehensive spelling reform of English has ever happened since: People can't be bothered with it.

Why should anyone who has mastered the cumbersome, illogical, yet historically revealing spelling system of the English language suddenly want to take the trouble to master a completely *new* system? The leaders of America after the Revolutionary War were no less influenced by this piece of common sense than millions of other writers and speakers of English have been.

In his *Spelling Book*, Webster states that he is specifically following Johnson's spelling, and he castigated attempts at any reform of English spelling in general, or American English spelling in particular. Webster even said he disapproved of one spelling modification that *was* establishing itself in America by the 1780s: the inclination to drop the *u* from words such as "honour" and "favour." Yet, strangely enough, with the money he made from *The American Spelling Book,* he launched himself into the spelling reform business. His next book, *Dissertations on the English Language,* published in 1789, called for a radical overhaul of the English spelling system. Later in his life, Webster withdrew from this extreme position, but many of his reformed spellings are included in his work, *An American Dictionary of the English Language,* published in 1828. In its first edition, 2,500 copies were published in the United States and 3,000 in England. The first edition took a year to sell out; generally, this book did not enjoy the success of *The American Spelling Book.* Still, it was a formidable work, containing about 70,000 entries (almost 30,000 more than Johnson had listed) and close to 40,000 definitions that had not appeared in any earlier dictionary.

Despite Webster's frequent disparagement of Johnson, the reality (which he might not have wanted to confront) was that he was greatly indebted to Johnson's great work. Many instances of his indebtedness are apparent both in Webster's definitions and in his illustrative quotations.

Webster recorded only those spellings already widely used by printers, so Webster cannot be said to have *established* a standard any more than Johnson did. Instead, like Johnson, Webster essentially *promoted* the standard. In particular, Webster's influence—like Johnson's—was primarily on the way people spelled in private correspondence, at least those people who would use his dictionary as a guide to currently acceptable spelling.

Still, there were differences between Johnson's objectives and Webster's. In particular, while Johnson looked at the printed material of his day and carefully stuck to the most common spelling of a word, Webster was led not only by a desire to promote a standard, but also by a wish to make American spelling distinct from British spelling. But despite his intensely nationalistic feelings, he did not in fact include in his dictionary very many of the revised spellings he recommended in his proposals for spelling reform. The general view of scholars is that Webster was reluctant to include too many of his revised spellings because he felt uneasy including them if there was no justification for them in current printing practice. On occasion, however, he decided to take a chance.

For example, Webster spelled the word "mould" as "mold" because he felt this was a perfectly reasonable simplification, as the word's vowel sound was identical to the vowel sound in words such as "old," "cold," and "gold"—which of course it is. Although there was no etymological justification for "mold," the form has stuck and today it is the usual way of spelling the word in America. As Donald Scragg asserts:

> In the sense that Webster was the first to differentiate between British and American usage, and in that it was frequently he who chose the variant of two spellings in early nineteenth-century use, which has subsequently been preferred in the United States, he can be said to have influenced the development of spelling. He is in a way "responsible" for such forms as "center," "color," and "defense."

An American Dictionary of the English Language was relatively unprofitable, and a revision Webster supervised in 1841 was not a success. After Webster's death in 1843, the rights to his dictionary were purchased from his estate by the brothers George and Charles Merriam, two astute businessmen from Springfield, Massachusetts. They employed Webster's son-in-law, who went by the name of Chauncey A. Goodrich, to produce a *good* new dictionary that would make them all *rich*. Goodrich worked hard on the new volume, which dispensed with many of Webster's more eccentric spellings and far-fetched etymologies.

The fruit of his work, published in 1847, was a comprehensive revision of Webster's dictionary. It was an instant success. A subsequent edition was published in 1864. The dictionary was further revised over a ten-year period and a completely new edition was published in 1890, entitled *Webster's International Dictionary*. It was followed in 1909 by *Webster's New International Dictionary*, which contained about 450,000 entries. A second edition of this was published in 1934, and further editions have been published since. Today, Merriam-Webster, Inc. (since 1964 a subsidiary of Encyclopædia Britannica, Inc.) is still the publisher of what remains the principal dictionary of American English.

A great deal of attention is paid at a spelling level to differences between American English and British English, but the differences are really rather trivial, and spoken and written English do not differ in significant respects between the United States and the United Kingdom. For the record, here are the main differences, today, between British English and American English spelling.

First, as we have seen, for British English words such as "colour," "favourite," and "honour," the *u* is dropped in the American English spellings: "color," "favorite," "honor." American English reverses the *-re* at the ends of some words to *-er,* such as for the spellings "center," "meter," and "theater"; it uses *ck* where some British words use *que* (for example, "cheque"/"check" and "chequer"/"checker"); and uses *g* where British English might use *gue* (such as "analogue"/"analog," "catalogue"/"catalog," and "dialogue"/ "dialog").

Where British English spellings use *s,* American

English tends to prefer *z;* examples are "analyze," "criticize," and "organization." Some British nouns, such as "defence" and "licence," are spelled with an *s* in the U.S.: "defense," "license." The *e* is dropped in the American spelling of certain words (for example, in "ageing" / "aging," "judgement"/"judgment," and "sizeable"/"sizable"), and words commonly spelled with *ae* or *oe* in Britain are simplified to have only the *e* in American English, as with "encyclopaedia"/"encyclopedia" and "manoeuvre"/ "maneuver." However, the U.S. spelling adds an *l* in certain spellings, such as for "enrolment"/"enrollment," "fulfil"/ "fulfill," and "skilful"/"skillful." Some other common words that differ in their British and U.S. spellings are: "jewellery"/"jewelry," "draught"/"draft," "pyjamas"/"pajamas," "plough"/"plow," "programme"/"program," and "tyre"/"tire."

In British English, verbs that end with a vowel and *l* usually double the *l* when *-ing* or *-ed* is added, but in American English the letter is not usually doubled—it is doubled only if the stress is on the second syllable. Some examples of the U.S. spelling are: "to counsel"/"counseling," "to equal"/ "equaling," "to model"/"modeling," "to quarrel"/ "quarreling," "to signal"/"signaled," and "to travel"/ "traveled."

Verbs such as "to dream," "to leap," and "to learn" are in British English spelled with the ending *-t* for the past tense ("dreamt," "leapt," and "learnt"), whereas American English spells them *-ed* ("dreamed," "leaped," "learned"). As we saw early in this book, British English likes "spelt" where American English prefers "spelled." However, where some British verbs add -*ed* (for example, "to fit"/"fitted," "to forecast"/"forecasted," and "to wed"/"wedded"), American English uses only the base form of the verb for the simple past (that is, "fit," "forecast," and "wed"). Another difference in the simple past is that where some verbs in British English end with -*ed* (for example, "to light"/"lighted," "to sneak"/"sneaked," "to strive"/"strived"), American English prefers an irregular spelling (respectively, "lit," "snuck," "strove").

American English is a wonderfully rich source of words and phrases that echo the sophisticated, energetic urban communities of the United States. There is wry wisdom in many of the expressions that have originated there, and it is hardly surprising that many British people use American English expressions to make themselves sound sophisticated, witty, and up to date.

Chapter 10

The Recent Past, the Present, and the Future

"Will B gr8 2 CU soon m8."—a form of ritten English ofen seen in the early twenty-first century, commonly usd by yunger people when communicating via an early form of interpersonal comtech, then nown as "text messaging." According to skolars, a translation of this sentence might be, "I anticipate deriving much plesure from a recurrence of our soshul intercorse in the near futur."

—Jake Bryson, *English Since 2001*
(published by Gates Global, Inc.,
A.D. 2125)

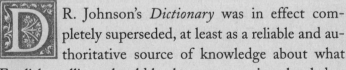

R. Johnson's *Dictionary* was in effect completely superseded, at least as a reliable and authoritative source of knowledge about what English spellings should be, by a great project that led to the creation of what was originally called a *New English Dictionary on Historical Principles* (*NED*), published in ten volumes from February 1, 1884, to April 19, 1928.

The purpose of the *NED* was to provide an inventory

of words in use in English since the mid–twelfth century, although it contains some words from before that time. In 1933 the *NED* was reissued as the *Oxford English Dictionary* (*OED*), published in twelve volumes; both the *NED* and *OED* were published by the Clarendon Press, Oxford, now part of Oxford University Press. The *OED* is not only easily the best and most comprehensive dictionary of the English language, but the best and most comprehensive dictionary of *any* language. It is a work of staggering complexity and breadth, and was from the outset a team effort. It is so vast a work that compilation of the third edition is still going on *today*, one and a half centuries since the project was first launched.

The research and collection of materials for the dictionary was first started in 1857 by the Philological Society of London. Editorial work began in 1879 when James Murray, president of the Philological Society, was appointed editor in chief. During his term as editor, Murray was responsible for approximately half of the dictionary, including the letters *A* to *D*, *H* to *K*, *O*, *P*, and *T*. Succeeding editors included Henry Bradley, William Alexander Craigie, and C. T. Onions, all illustrious scholars.

The policy of the *OED* is uncompromising: to attempt to record all known uses and variants of a word in *all* varieties of English, worldwide, past and present. As the 1933 Preface to the *OED* put it:

If there is any truth in the old Greek maxim that a large book is a great evil, English dictionaries have been steadily growing worse ever since their inception more than three centuries ago. To set Cawdrey's slim small volume of 1604 beside the completed Oxford Dictionary of 1933 is like placing the original acorn beside the oak that has grown out of it.

The Preface goes on to state the objective of the 1933 *OED*:

> ... to present in alphabetical series the words that have formed the English vocabulary from the time of the earliest records down to the present day, with all the relevant facts concerning their form, sense-history, pronunciation, and etymology. It embraces not only the standard language of literature and conversation, whether current at the moment, or obsolete, or archaic, but also the main technical vocabulary, and a large measure of dialectal usage and slang.

A Supplement to the Oxford English Dictionary, which recorded words that had come into use in the English-speaking world after the preparation of the *OED*, was begun in 1955 under the editorial direction of R. W. Burchfield. It was published by the Clarendon Press in four volumes between 1972 and 1986.

The second edition of the *Oxford English Dictionary*, known as *OED2*, was published in twenty volumes in 1989 by the Oxford University Press. Its coeditors were John A. Simpson and Edmund S. C. Weiner. It included in one alphabetical sequence all the words defined in the original twelve-volume *OED* as well as supplementary volumes. A CD-ROM version of the *OED2* was first issued in 1992.

The full-size second edition contains about 2,400,000 illustrative quotations from English literature and other written records which are used to support the definitions of words. The full-size *OED* fills an entire bookshelf, and is a work for a public or private library, but Oxford University Press has ingeniously come up with many abbreviated versions of the main work. My personal favorite is the *Shorter Oxford English Dictionary*, which focuses mainly on words used since 1700 (just yesterday in *OED* terms). This shorter version is still two volumes long and has 3,801 pages, but at least one can lift its two volumes from the bookshelf without ending up in a hospital's emergency room.

Here are some interesting facts about the second edition of the *OED* (the figures should be regarded as approximate):

Size: 20 volumes, 21,730 pages
Weight of a full set of 20 volumes: 62.6 kg or 137.72 lb
Amount of ink used to print complete run: 2,830 kg or 6,243 lb
Number of words in entire text: 59 million
Number of printed characters: 350 million
Number of entries: 291,500
Number of main entries: 231,100
Longest entry: the verb "set," with over 430 senses and consisting of approximately 60,000 words or 326,000 characters (the length of an average novel)

Number of cross-reference entries: 60,400

Number of cross-references within entries: 580,600

Number of pronunciations: 139,900

Number of etymologies: 219,800

Number of quotations (from English literature and records): 2,436,600

Most frequently quoted work (in various full and partial versions, and translations): Bible (approx. 25,000 quotations)

Most frequently quoted single author: Shakespeare (approximately 33,300 quotations)

Most frequently quoted single work by Shakespeare: Hamlet (almost 1,600 quotations)

Percentage of quotations by centuries:

20th century	20%
19th century	31%
18th century	11%
17th century	16%
16th century	10%
15th century	4.5%
14th century	3.5%
13th century	1%
1st to 12th centuries	1%
Undated*	0.5%

---

* "Undated" includes approximately 1,250 quotations from *Beowulf,* with the balance consisting of proverbs, nursery rhymes, "made-up" examples, and references to the appearance of word-forms in other dictionaries.

James Essinger

The confident and ambitious scope of the project that led to the creation of the *NED,* and later the *OED,* reflects the fact that by 1857 English spelling had been fixed for more than enough time for the creators of the planned new dictionary not to have to give any thought to whether English spelling was stable enough to support such an enterprise. Today, with really only a small number of exceptions, the correct spelling of English words is, *in principle,* agreed throughout the English-speaking world, given the differences in British and American usage already noted. In the vast majority of cases, there is no choice. You either spell the word correctly according to the accepted standard or you don't. There is no room for compromise here: Either you get the word right or you get it wrong.

There are other influential English dictionaries, of course. People often have their own dictionaries they prefer, and any such preference is perfectly valid as long as the dictionary is a respected one. But remember: Dictionaries reflect usage, they don't (and they shouldn't) *dictate* usage.

I say above that *in principle* most spellings are agreed throughout the English-speaking world, but there are exceptions. A few words do have alternative spellings, and this remains the case even after the continuing intensive movement toward standardization that has prevailed since around 1700. The decision whether or not to include an *e* in words like "usage," "aging," and "judgment" is to some extent a matter of personal taste. Another area where there remains surprisingly little agreement is whether you should use a single or double consonant in words like "benefiting" or "focusing." In many cases both options are allowed. There is also an increasing tendency to spell "farther" as "further," although traditionalists (including myself) continue to prefer to distinguish in the spelling between the geographical "farther" and the purely conceptual "further." Also, there are no standardized spellings for the names of the letters in the English alphabet apart from "zee."

In fact, careful examination of different dictionaries shows that many have different preferences on whether certain compound words are hyphenated, spaced, or put together as one word. For example, the Collins series of dictionaries lists "kickback" (noun), "kick back" (verb), "kick-start" (verb), and "kick turn" (noun). The spelling of such word compounds is almost inevitably a matter offering the opportunity for some personal preference. Because—again—dictionaries only record usage, there will inevitably be disagreement or inconsistencies between different dictionaries when usage itself has not yet solidified. The general tendency seems to be to avoid using the hyphen once the use of the compound becomes more established. For example, Jane Austen, writing in the early nineteenth century, wrote "to-day" but today we do indeed write "today." Similarly, "week-end" would probably be regarded as pedantic nowadays when "weekend" is so firmly established, but during the nineteenth century "week-end" was the most common form. I can't really see how anyone can legislate on words such as "kick back," "kick-back," or "kickback" because all these spellings are eminently reasonable. Many of the new words that have come into English in recent decades ("skyjack," to take just one example) are compound words, partly because they seem to be popular with newspaper headline writers. Sometimes a particular spelling will quickly gain prominence (in this case *OED* prefers "skyjack" as a single word, and this is probably most often seen), but often a compound word will be used in a hyphenated, single word, or separate word-form and really no one has the right to say that any of them are "right" or "wrong." The fact that in the spelling even of a language as widely spoken throughout the world as English there are gray areas demonstrates that writing, like any other technology, is never a perfect tool.

When I was planning *Spellbound* I intended to provide a section about the efforts that have been made over the years to reform English spelling. But as the book progressed this idea seemed increasingly irrelevant.

All attempts to reform English spelling have one thing in common: They are failures. There have been many different kinds of attempts over the years—from people who have advocated replacing the letters of the English alphabet with completely new letters that purport more accurately to set down the phonemes of the English language; to less ambitious schemes that try to introduce more regularity and consistency into how English vowel sounds and consonant sounds are represented; to small reforms proposed in the spellings of particular words. The writer George Bernard Shaw (1856–1950) was a keen advocate of spelling reform, and due to his great success as a playwright was able to demand that his printers impose some of them on his readers. For example, he insisted that words such as "haven't" and "don't" were printed without apostrophes as "havent" and "dont": Don't ask me why. He was also partial to the older spelling of "show" as "shew," which makes little sense as it actually introduces illogicality since *ow* is a more common use of the diphthong to represent that sound. When he died, he left a legacy to fund a competition to design a new, universal alphabet that would not be based around the usual letters of English at all.

Those would-be reformers who have suggested replacing English letters with a new alphabet seem to me, frankly, completely bananas. Of course, one *could* develop a new alphabet for English, and really quite easily, such as by turning letters upside down or by inventing new ones. But the only possible justification for creating a new alphabet for English would be to define the forty-four phonemes of English with complete regularity and precision, and the International Phonetic Alphabet does this very well, except that—as you'll recall from the example I offered—no one is really likely to want written English to look like *that*. Plus, as I've argued throughout this book, the historical story of English spelling is an important and interesting part of our cultural heritage, and it seems a shame to lose it. Indeed it seems a crime to deprive our children of it and oblige them to learn instead some strange, recently invented new alphabet that doesn't even look like the tried and tested Roman one.

As regards the "middle" range of would-be reformers—that is, those who suggest radical but logical reforms of the consistency of English spelling—the big problem with all their efforts is that the results look horrible. They seem unfamiliar, alien, and give the appearance of being deliberately contrived to annoy and bewilder us.

Why is this? Partly because the very process of learning to read and write in the conventional way makes us alert to major mistakes, and these middle-ranking types of spelling reform simply look like major mistakes. It's true that most of us have some particular spelling bugbears, but surely the way to deal with that problem is to learn to spell the words properly rather than flattering oneself that one's mis-spelling is somehow a useful idiosyncrasy, when it isn't.

At the heart of *Spellbound* there are ultimately two principal arguments, and they help to explain why these middle-ranking spelling reforms have never worked and are not likely to do so.

First, as we have seen, experienced readers read by making very rapid, even almost instinctive, association be-tween the way a word looks on the page and a particular meaning. This being so, the illogicality of English spelling is not necessarily a major problem once the spelling sys-tem of English has actually been learned.

Second, and to make the point yet again, a new way of spelling that utilizes the Roman alphabet would, for perhaps no really significant benefits, deprive us of the rich cultural heritage represented by the current English spelling system. The English writing system is, in effect, a daily reminder of the heritage of the English-speaking people, and we have every right to be extremely proud of it.

Which does not mean that there is no scope *at all* for effecting gentle improvements in the efficiency of the English writing system. Put another way, there may well be words whose spelling can usefully be modified over time.

In many other alphabetic and logographic languages of the world, spelling reform has been more successful. Over the past century, just to take three examples, the spelling of Russian, Chinese, and German have all been reformed. The last ratification of a reform of German spelling was issued as recently as 1996. However, the English spelling system has a curiously robust conservatism about it, and it really is very difficult to imagine not *how* the English spelling system could be reformed, but that anybody would be bothered to use the reformed version. On the whole, attempted spelling reforms of the English spelling system have never been anything more than a series of dead ends in the story of spelling.

And so we come to the present day... and beyond. What developments in the spelling of English are going on today, and what developments are likely to appear in the future? Would a book about English published a century from now feature some of the gently simplified spellings lightheartedly suggested at the very start of this chapter— but still feel itself culturally superior to the drastic abbreviations of text messaging today?

Now, in the first decade of the twenty-first century, English is not only the closest the planet has to a world language, but is becoming even more important in this respect. Most educated people around the world, no matter what their mother tongue might be, regard the ability to read and write in English as an element of their education. English has become the de facto language of the Internet and of global business, and in many respects it is also the language of global culture. The Internet has undoubtedly boosted the international importance of English even beyond the heights it had already reached by the mid-1990s, which was when the Internet's massive and to an extent all-pervading influence first began to make itself felt. English has become a world language of unprecedented significance and status: a very far cry indeed from the days when Shakespeare wrote his plays; days when English was spoken only in England by a population that at the time numbered barely four million people.

English words have been borrowed comprehensively by many languages, and there is a tendency nowadays for English borrowings to be used and retained very much as they are rather than adapted into the spelling and pronunciation of the "host" language or "translated" into a form more acceptable to the host speakers. The reason for this particular development is that the British English—or, which is more often the case, American English—culture has acquired a significance and status that makes it attractive for non–English speakers to use English words as a kind of conscious cultural status symbol. For example, the English word "baby," which is used both by English-speakers and in popular culture to indicate someone for whom one has affection, is used in many languages to indicate this without being translated into the native language's own context.

Today, English is spoken as a native language by about 350,000,000 people worldwide. Most speakers live in one of the following countries: the United States, the United Kingdom, Canada, Australia, New Zealand, South Africa, and Ireland. It is not known precisely how many people speak English as their second language, but the number is certainly well in excess of one billion. In terms of numbers of native speakers, English ranks fourth among the languages of the world after Mandarin Chinese, Hindi, and Spanish. However, when it comes to the number of second-language-speakers, there is no competition.

English is also by far the most important international scientific, academic, and commercial language. Its penetration in the realms of science and academia is so extensive that in many universities where English is not the main language of instruction, it is routine for graduate students to write their theses in the English language.

It is not always appreciated by people living outside Africa that English plays an enormously important role in that continent. For example, English functions as an official language of administration in Botswana, Kenya, Lesotho, Malawi, Swaziland, Uganda, Zambia, and Zimbabwe. It is the language of instruction at Makerere University in Kampala, Uganda, at the University of Nairobi, Kenya, and at the University of Dar es Salaam in Tanzania. The West African states of Gambia, Ghana, Nigeria, and Sierra Leone all have English as their official language. The official language of Liberia is also English. Indigenous African languages compete very healthily with English and the other former colonial language, French, but English has a massively important role in Africa, just as it does in India.

What kind of influences are likely to be important as far as how English spelling may change in the future?

Newspapers usually punctuate and spell well enough, but they are prone to using abbreviations which the great Dr. Johnson would certainly have found confusing. While researching *Spellbound* I have often noted down curiosities that I have seen, and this one is a heading from a newspaper sports section:

7-wkt Matt ko's Boks

This, as will be immediately apparent to readers familiar with the sport, is a reference to a cricketer with the Christian name of Matt who took seven wickets ("7-wkt") against the South African cricket team the Springboks ("Boks"), with the result that they lost the match. The word "ko's" is derived from "knock out" (or "knockout") and so this means "Seven-wicket Matt knocks out the Springboks." This example demonstrates the extraordinary and understandable willingness of modern newspapers to try to sum up the content of a headline not only in the fewest possible words, but in the fewest possible *letters*.

When you look at a copy of a newspaper from the early twentieth century or even earlier, you do not see the same willingness to make headlines short, which is why old newspapers frequently seem as though they were written by novelists being paid by the word. Incidentally, one consequence of the desire among newspaper editors to make headlines as short as possible is that one particular word that is actually obsolete in spoken English is regularly used in newspaper headlines: the verb "to wed," as in the headline "Charles to wed Camilla." It's an interesting example of how a written form of a language keeps an obsolete word alive because it is nice and short. There seems little doubt that newspapers will continue to play a key role in influencing the future of certain types of spellings, especially relating to abbreviations.

If it really *is* abbreviations you want, check out the American entertainment magazine *Variety*, which takes a positive pride in the obscurity and brevity of its headlines. Written for entertainment insiders, half the point of the headlines is that they are incomprehensible to people

outside the business. During the mid-1990s, *Variety* printed
the following headline:

Biz pix POG flix

To understand this you have to know that "biz" is an
abbreviated way of writing "showbiz" or "show business."
You have to know that *Variety* habitually spells (at least in
headings) words that end in *-cks* as *-x,* and therefore "pix"
means "picks." You also need to know that "POG" was the
acronym for a particular rooming house in Hollywood
that was home to a group of talented, young male screen-
writers and known colloquially as Pad o' Guys, or POG.
Finally, you need to know that "flix" is of course *Variety*-
speak for "flicks" or "movies," with the nickname coming
from the fact that in the early days movies used to flicker
on the screen when they were being viewed. Therefore, the
headline translated into English might read: "Hollywood
is choosing to make movies written by members of the
writing fraternity known as the Pad of Guys."

Like the shortening of headlines, something that seems
to be a clear trend in the spelling of English is the ever-
increasing popularity of acronyms. It's not precisely clear
when this development began to manifest itself, but it
seems largely to have been nurtured during the 1940s by a
wartime atmosphere of austerity and a need for brevity.
When Thomas Watson created International Business
Machines in 1925, he called it precisely that. But by the

SPELLBOUND

1940s the organization was being called IBM and nobody would refer to it as "International Business Machines" any longer unless they were writing a history of it.

In his famous essay on the fictional language "Newspeak," the language of the ruling elite in his novel *Nineteen Eighty-Four* (1949), George Orwell points out that acronyms tend to appeal to political bodies wishing to create a sense of a compact and focused methodology as opposed to a more idealistic entity:

In the Ministry of Truth, for example, the Records Department, in which Winston Smith worked, was called *Recdep*, the Fiction Department was called *Ficdep*, the Teleprogrammes Department was called *Teledep*, and so on. This was not done solely with the object of saving time. Even in the early decades of the twentieth century, telescoped words and phrases had been one of the characteristic features of political language; and it had been noticed that the tendency to use abbreviations of this kind was most marked in totalitarian countries and totalitarian organizations.

Examples were such words as *Nazi, Gestapo, Comintern, Inprecorr, Agitprop*. In the beginning the practice had been adopted as it were instinctively, but in Newspeak it was used with a conscious purpose. It was perceived that in thus abbreviating a name one narrowed and subtly altered its meaning, by cutting out most of the associations that would otherwise cling to it. The words *Communist International*, for instance, call up a composite picture of universal human brotherhood, red flags, barricades, Karl Marx, and the Paris Commune. The word *Comintern*, on the other hand, suggests merely a tightly-knit organization and a well-defined body of doctrine. It refers to something almost as easily recognized, and as limited in purpose, as a chair or a table. *Comintern* is a word that can be uttered almost without taking thought, whereas *Communist International* is a phrase over which one is obliged to linger at least momentarily.

What Orwell says here could also apply to corporate bodies. I can certainly think of many cases where a large corporation has embarked on a major new branding that in essence is little more than a conversion of a long name into an acronym.

Might the tendency in favor of acronyms also lead to a tendency to shorten the spelling of English words without altering their appearance so dramatically that they look repugnant? Might the kind of mild modifications suggested (not entirely seriously) at the start of this chapter become current at some point in the future?

Dropping obviously redundant "silent" letters, such as the *k* at the start of "known," might be the kind of development that may happen in a world where the sheer number of nonnative speakers mastering English spelling could one day create pressure even on its prized traditions. But there is no sign of such a development happening now. In fact, it is not even easy to point to many other no-ticeable trends in English spelling except, perhaps, the feeling even in Britain that words such as "judgement" (or "acknowledgement") might be better off without that *e* before the suffix, as they are in America. There remains confusion about whether words such as "focusing" or "benefiting"—an issue I've mentioned already—should be spelled with one or two consonants before the *-ing,* and while British and American usage sometimes differ here, the truth is that there is no widely agreed standard and both forms are acceptable in most cases. Even computer spell-checks often disagree on this particular issue, but that shouldn't surprise us because computer spell-checks are based around whatever dictionary the software de-signer regarded as a useful source and, as we have seen, dictionaries differ.

Two major developments in communications that have proliferated greatly since the dawn of the twenty-first century are the use of electronic mail and sending text messages on mobile telephones. The very spelling of the word "e-mail" is in something of a state of flux, with no standard yet evolved—"email" also seems entirely accept-able. In 1994 the Collins dictionary listed the spelling "e-mail," but the 2000 edition lists "e mail," "e-mail," or "email," while *OED* lists both "email" and "e-mail." There is, I think, an increasing tendency for the hyphen to be dropped in accordance with the slimmed-down and func-tional way people tend to communicate today.

The great increase in the importance of e-mail over the

past few years is a fascinating development. Most people in business today spend much of their time—often several hours a day—on-line and dealing with their e-mails takes up a lot of their time; indeed, some people do little else. The curious thing, it seems to me, is that the quality of spelling used in e-mails is surprisingly traditional. It is not as if some particular spelling style has evolved for e-mails, and in fact I know of several businesspeople who have told me they regard a spelling mistake or typo in an e-mail from a supplier as a serious error that devalues the supplier in their eyes. There seems little choice but to conclude that, no matter how high-tech e-mails may be, they are by and large regarded by the people who write and read them as simply another form of correspondence and require an adherence to usual spelling conventions.

Ironically, one consequence of our massive use of e-mail is that the lost art of written correspondence has to a considerable extent been rediscovered. Technology is, after all, merely a means to an end, and most of us enjoy e-mail contact with people we like.

Mobile phone texting is a rather more complex matter from a spelling perspective. I've asked many people about their approach to spelling in text messages and found that attitudes vary considerably from one person to the next. Most people I know who do use texting on occasion as part of their business and professional lives tend to be fairly formal in their written communications by this method and spell pretty much as they would in a letter or an e-mail. But most of us use mobile texting mainly for personal communications.

Many people, particularly younger ones, delight in employing a wide variety of shorter forms of words when they text their friends. There is a built-in commercial justification here: The longer the text message is, the more it costs. Users are charged for each message sent, with a limit of around fifty words, including spaces, per message. When the text exceeds that, the message is broken into parts and each part is sent and charged as a separate item—so using shortened word-forms means you can fit more into a single message, at a lower cost.

Many of these shorter word-forms, in fact, essentially echo logographic types of writing systems that remind us of the hieroglyphic origin of many of our letters. For example, spelling the word "mate" as "m8," "great" as "gr8," or "see you" as "CU" are a kind of English-language hieroglyph or Chinese character. It seems a strange way to write, and I certainly wouldn't do it myself; but then I'm in my late forties and people who spell text in this way probably aren't.

Indeed, I'm probably a bad example of mobile text spelling because I use predictive text and tend to spell words pretty much in their standard form. But several of my friends are happy to use shortened forms of words such as "tmrw" for "tomorrow," "msg" for "message," and "pics" for "pictures" or photographs. One should surely not be too draconian about these abbreviations, which after all are used when sending messages by a technology that strongly reinforces the need for brevity.

This said, the use of predictive text is a powerful force in favor of conventional spellings because you don't need laboriously to pick out each letter as you used to have to do. The phone is programmed to recognize keypad combinations as particular words and automatically display them for you. It is also possible to "teach" your mobile phone's program new words or names that you want to be able to use, so that those words appear automatically when you enter the corresponding keypad combination. However, some people teach their predictive text program abbreviated or nonstandard spellings, which obviously tends to promote the use of these spellings.

The lesson from all of this seems to me clear. The fact that we have evolved new types of technology that Alfred the Great would scarcely have been able to imagine does not alter the fact that ultimately we are as influenced as he was by a desire to be part of the spelling standard that belongs to our cultural heritage. Our attachment to this standard is even stronger than we can imagine, and in a very real sense it masters us and governs us rather than vice versa. And remember how popular the National Spelling Bee is, and how that promotes—even exults—in traditional spellings, especially if they are tricky ones? On the whole, I doubt English spelling will be reformed by the momentum of new technology.

Today, in our endlessly complex and apparently endlessly sophisticated high-tech world, we may be temporarily spellbound by new technology, but our marvel and wonder at it tend to wear off quite soon. Our marvel and wonder at our heritage as users of the English spelling system, however, have not worn off in 1,500 years and surely never shall. We are destined to be spellbound by English spelling forever.

BIBLIOGRAPHY

Adkins, Lesley and Roy. *The Keys of Egypt: The Race to Read the Hieroglyphs.* HarperCollins (UK), 2001.

Andrews, Carol. *The Rosetta Stone.* The British Museum Press (UK), 2004.

Bragg, Melvyn. *The Adventure of English: The Biography of a Language.* Sceptre (UK), 2003.

Bryson, Bill. *Mother Tongue.* Penguin Books (UK), 1991.

Burgess, Anthony. *Language Made Plain.* Fontana (UK), 1974.

Chisholm, Kate. "Dr. Johnson's Way with Words." *Sunday Telegraph*, April 3, 2005.

Collier, Mark, and Bill Manley. *How to Read Egyptian Hieroglyphs.* The British Museum Press (UK), 2004.

Cook, Vivian. *Accomodating Brocolli in the Cemetary: Or Why Can't Anybody Spell?* Profile Books (UK), 2004.

Crystal, David. *Encyclopaedia of the English Language.* Cambridge University Press (UK), 2003.

DeFrancis, John. *Visible Speech: The Diverse Oneness of Writing Systems.* Honolulu: University of Hawaii Press, 1989.

Hogg, Richard M., ed. *The Cambridge History of the English Language.* Cambridge University Press (UK), 1999.

Parkinson, R. B. (ed.). *The Tale of Sinuhe: And Other Ancient Egyptian Poems, 1940–1640 B.C.* Oxford University Press (UK), 1998.

Parkinson, Richard. *Cracking Codes: The Rosetta Stone and Decipherment.* The British Museum Press (UK), 1999.

Radcliffe, Zane. *The Killer's Guide to Iceland.* Black Swan (UK), 2005.

Sacks, David. *The Alphabet: Unravelling the Mystery of the Alphabet from A to Z.* Arrow Books (UK), 2004.

Sampson, Geoffrey. *Writing Systems.* Stanford, California: Stanford University Press, 1985.

Schmandt-Besserat, Denise. *How Writing Came About.* Austin, Texas: University of Texas Press, 1996.

Scragg, D. G. *A History of English Spelling.* Manchester University Press (UK), 1974

Stearns, Macdonald, Jr. *Crimean Gothic Analysis and Etymology of the Corpus.* Anna Libri & Co. (UK), 1978.

Truss, Lynne. *Eats, Shoots & Leaves.* Profile Books (UK), 2003.

Walker, C. B. F. *Cuneiform.* The British Museum Press (UK), 2004.

Willans, Geoffrey, and Ronald Searle. *Molesworth.* Penguin Books (UK), 1999.

ACKNOWLEDGMENTS

Many people gave me their time very generously when I was researching this book. I am grateful to them all, and particularly to Mairi Allan of the Natural History Museum in London; Sir Christopher Ball; Claris Chan; Kate Chisholm; Professor Matti Leiwo of Jyväskylä University; Nigel Roche of St. Bride Printing Library; Professor Geoffrey Sampson; Professor Donald Scragg; Chris Stringer of the Natural History Museum in London; and the cultural historian Professor Stephen Walton.

Margaret Dowley, M.B.E., helped me immeasurably with preparing the text and made many suggestions for improving it, all of which I took up with embarrassing enthusiasm. Thank you, Margaret, for your patience, calmness (a quality I have all too often lacked when we've worked together), and good sense.

I am also extremely grateful to the expert Egyptologist Dr. Richard Parkinson and his colleagues Dr. Nigel

Strudwick and Dr. Marcel Maree in the Department of Egyptology at the British Museum in London for the quality of their scholarship, vast knowledge of Egyptian hieroglyphs, and willingness to impart some of this knowledge to me.

My gratitude to Jeremy Robson of Robson Books and also to his colleague Jennifer Lansbury, who edited this book so well. Barbara Phelan of Robson Books also played a vital role in producing this book. My thanks to Caitlin Alexander and her colleagues at Bantam Dell for their hard work on the U.S. edition.

My gratitude also to my friend Clair-Marie, the Lynne Truss of accurate spelling; to Margot Charlton at the Oxford Word and Language Service; to Jenny Drake; to Eddie Jephcott and Elton Butcher for many interesting conversations about language; to Mike Kinder for getting me interested in Latin; to Richard Curtis and Ben Elton for their brilliant if not entirely true-to-life characterization of the great Dr. Johnson in *Blackadder* (a masterly episode even if they were wrong about Johnson not listing "savsage"); and to Caroline, Oliver, India, and Caspar Latham for their enthusiasm for the idea of this book when it was still in the planning stage, and particularly to India for being so sure about the title.

My sincere thanks to W.M., for reminding me what really matters, and to Joe M., whose great enthusiasm for languages was a real inspiration when I was writing this book: Congratulations on what you have achieved so far,

Joe, and may your range of scholarship eventually rival Augier Ghislain de Busbecq's.

For personal reasons, my thanks to Dr. David Lythall, to Kieran Minshull of L.K. Leon & Co., and also to Dr. Simon Ellis, Sue Brown, Nigel Andrew, C. Steven Bailey, Jennie Bailey, and Wallace Poon.

My thanks to my colleague Helen Wylie for her help with so many aspects of this book—in particular the research, the final editing, the collation of the illustrations, and preparing the index. My great thanks also to Stephen Gillatt for his extensive help and support. And as always, my great thanks to Sheila Ableman, queen of literary agents, for understanding what I was trying to do with this book and for finding a home for it.

Finally, an offering of the sincerest gratitude to my subject matter in *Spellbound*: the English language. It is a language I am privileged to have as my mother tongue due solely to the fact that, in 1939, barely two months before the outbreak of World War II, Britain offered a safe haven to my father Theodore from Nazi Germany. I am proud to write a book about the spelling of the English language, that most precious possession of the English-speaking world, a world which very literally enabled me to exist. My father died while this book was in preparation: I dedicate it to him with love and admiration. Good night, sweet prince.

James Essinger, 2007

INDEX

INDEX

INDEX

ABOUT THE AUTHOR

James Essinger is an Oxford graduate who has published more than thirty books. He is particularly interested in the history of ideas that have had a practical impact on the modern world. His previous writings and his time spent teaching English abroad leave him exceptionally well qualified in the linguistic field.